The Big Blue Book

25 multi-purpose outlines
for pre-school groups

Scripture Union

Scripture Union, 207–209 Queensway, Bletchley, MK2 2EB, England.

Scripture Union is an international Christian charity working with churches in more than 130 countries providing resources to bring the good news about Jesus Christ to children, young people and families – and to encourage them to develop spiritually through the Bible and prayer.

As well as a network of volunteers, staff and associates who run holidays, church-based events and school Christian groups, Scripture Union produces a wide range of publications and supports those who use the resources through training programmes.

Email: info@scriptureunion.org.uk

Internet: www.scriptureunion.org.uk

© Scripture Union 2002

First published 2002; reprinted 2006, 2007

ISBN 978 1 85999 657 7

Scripture Union Australia, Locked Bag 2, Central Coast Business Centre, NSW 2252, Australia

Website: www.scriptureunion.org.au

Scripture Union USA, PO Box 987, Valley Forge, PA 19482, USA
Website: www.scriptureunion.org

Performing Licence

If you wish to perform any of the material in this book, you are free to do so without charge, providing the performance is undertaken in an amateur context. The purchase of this book constitutes a licence granting the right to perform the pieces for no financial gain. Those wishing to engage in commercial or professional performances should make a separate approach in writing to Scripture Union.

Unless otherwise stated, Bible quotations are from the Contemporary English Version © American Bible Society, published by HarperCollins Publishers, with kind permission from the British and Foreign Bible Society.

British Library Cataloguing-in-Publication Data: a catalogue record for this book is available from the British Library.

Acknowledgements

Thank you to Christine Orme and Christine Wood for permission to use copyright material from *Splash*, SU 1992.

Some activities are based on material previously published in *Sing, Say and Move, Jigsaw, Let's join in, Let's Praise and Pray, Let's Sing and Shout!* and *Let's all clap hands!* © Scripture Union.

Thank you to Diana Turner and Jackie Cray for so much valuable support and constructive comment.

A note on Music books	
JP	Junior Praise (Marshall Pickering)
JU	Jump Up If You're Wearing Red (NS/CHP)
KS	Kidsource (Kevin Mayhew)
GTB	Gospelling to the Beat (Scripture Union Australia)

Series editors: Maggie Barfield, Sarah Mayers

Consultant editor: Penny Boshoff

Desk editor: Nina Palmer

Editorial support: Lizzie Green

Writers: Judith Wigley, Judith Merrell, Gillian Thomson, Denise Niel, Jo Bailey, Lynn Huggins-Cooper

Additional material: Maggie Barfield, Christine O'Brien, Rachael Champness, Marjory Francis, Mary Houlgate, Margaret Perkins, Angela Thompson

Cover and internal design by Mark Carpenter Design Consultants

Illustrations: Claire Vessey

Printed and bound in Great Britain by
Marston Book Services Limited, Oxfordshire

Contents

Welcome to Tiddlywinks...

Remember the game? Play it anywhere, anytime with almost any age. It can be a two-minute time filler or an afternoon of family fun captivating even the youngest child's attention. Flipping, flying coloured discs, furious scrambles after lost 'winks' and triumphant laughter as three-year-old Lucy beats Granddad again! It's so simple, such fun.

Welcome to *Tiddlywinks*... resource material for young children that's fun, flexible, and extremely user-friendly.

Fun because it's child and therefore 'play' centred. The material reflects the understanding that young children grow, develop and learn through play. *Tiddlywinks* provides young children with a wide range of enjoyable, stimulating play experiences as a basis for learning about themselves, the world in which they live and the God who made both them and that world. It's designed to be good fun!

Flexible because it is adaptable to almost any situation. The work of the Christian church is no longer restricted to Sundays as literally thousands of carers and their young children flock through the doors of our churches, halls, and community buildings between Monday and Friday. Thankfully church leaders are waking up to the fact that what happens midweek really matters, and these people are being increasingly valued as members of the extended church family. That in no way devalues the very important work that goes on during a Sunday, both within the framework of a service of worship or Sunday teaching group. BOTH Sunday and midweek work are important and of equal value, but material that's easily adaptable to a variety of different contexts needs to be flexible. *Tiddlywinks* has been written and designed with that flexibility in mind. Whether you are responsible for a midweek carer and toddler group, pram service (more likely to be called something like Butterflies, Minnows or Little Angels!), or you are a leader in a playgroup or nursery class, overseeing a Sunday crèche, teaching an early years Sunday group class, or part of a community based play centre or shoppers' crèche – there is material in *Tiddlywinks* that will be adaptable to your situation. Some of you will be looking to fill a two-hour programme, others two minutes! *Tiddlywinks'* pick-and-mix style is here to meet the needs of a wide range of contexts.

User-friendly because it is accessible to leaders who are just starting out as well as those with more experience. Whether you're wondering how to tell a Bible story, wanting to learn age-appropriate rhymes and songs, looking for creative ideas for prayer or wondering how telling the story of Noah might fit in with your early learning goals, *Tiddlywinks* can help you.

Tiddlywinks places great importance upon relationships. It recognises the crucial role of parents, carers and leaders in the development of a young child in his or her early years and the need to support and encourage all who share in this important task. Friendship between adults and children creates community, identity and a sense of belonging. When that community becomes a safe place where trust and friendship grow, both adults and children thrive within it. There could be no better foundation in the life of a young child.

OK, but you still have questions:

Each outline has an activity page which can be used either in the group or at home. Photocopy as many pages as you need. Some of the craft activities recommended on these pages will work better if you photocopy them directly onto thin card instead of onto paper. Encourage adults to talk about the leaflets with the children and to do the activities together.

If the sheet is taken home, you could use the blank reverse to photocopy your group news or notices onto.

Where do I start…? How do I use it…? Who can use it…? Where can it be used…? When is the best time…? Why introduce spiritual topics to young children at all…? Do I need special equipment…? What skills will I need…? Will it cost anything…? Who will come…?

Everyone who has worked with young children has asked these and many other questions at some stage! The writers of *Tiddlywinks* are firmly

convinced that adults learn through experience too. In fact, 'hands-on' is the very best way to learn! No academic or paper qualification can replace first hand experience of simply being and engaging with young children as they play and learn. The best qualifications for working with young children, are a desire to be with them and a willingness to learn.

The following pages are here to help you think through questions you may have, guide your planning and preparation and help you get the best for your children from *Tiddlywinks*. We start with the all-important question WHY? If you are convinced of the reasons for working with young children, developing body, mind and spirit, you will keep going even when it feels tough. Conviction produces commitment and determination, qualities worth cultivating in any children's leader. And *Tiddlywinks* is here to help. Enjoy it!

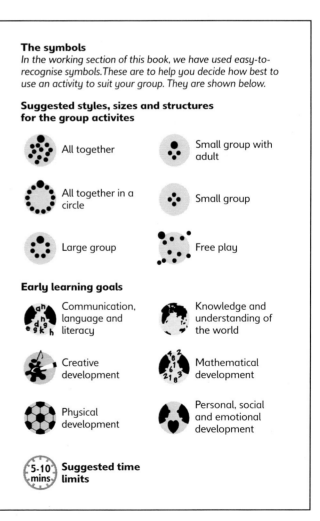

The symbols
In the working section of this book, we have used easy-to-recognise symbols. These are to help you decide how best to use an activity to suit your group. They are shown below.

Suggested styles, sizes and structures for the group activites

All together

Small group with adult

All together in a circle

Small group

Large group

Free play

Early learning goals

Communication, language and literacy

Knowledge and understanding of the world

Creative development

Mathematical development

Physical development

Personal, social and emotional development

5-10 mins — **Suggested time limits**

Why?

Why work with babies, toddlers and pre-schoolers? Why go to such lengths to provide appropriate play facilities, resources and materials for such young children? Let's be honest; they are noisy, messy, sometimes smelly, and thoroughly exhausting!

But, as the psalmist reminds us, they are also very special, a gift from God:

*You are the one who put me together
inside my mother's body,
and I praise you
because of the wonderful
      way you created me.*

(Psalm 139:13,14)

Few of us would deny the wonder of a new baby. The sense of miracle is often overwhelming and awe inspiring, and it isn't difficult to believe in a Creator God at such times. But the real truth behind the psalmist's words is that God's mark is upon each and every one of us right from the very beginning. From conception each one is a unique, individual human being, made in the image of God.

God's image within us is spiritual, and children (especially young children), are spiritual beings in their own right. As leaders, parents or carers of young children God gives us the awesome responsibility of sharing in his creation process. As the children in our care grow in body, mind and spirit, we become partners with God in that developmental process. Research tells us that the first five years of a child's life are the most crucial, laying down important foundations for the rest of life. If that is so, we know that we face quite a challenge. The stimulus we provide, the environment in which they grow, the quality of relationships and the values they experience will make an enormous difference to the children in our care.

Good relationships between young children and their carers are crucial for healthy growth and development. A child who experiences love, trust, security and forgiveness in their closest human relationships will quickly understand about the God who also loves, cherishes, protects and forgives them. When they become part of a community that lives out those values the impact is even greater. Their experience will make sense of all they will come to learn through the many Bible stories they hear; stories that reflect those same values and truths. When a group both practices and teaches these values it becomes a powerful place of spiritual learning for all who are part of that community. Young children and their parents and carers will thrive and grow in body, mind and spirit.

When fostered at an early age the relationship between a young child and God is transparently beautiful, often uncomplicated and spontaneous. Children are often more in touch with their spirituality than adults. They sense, they feel, they wonder but don't necessarily express those things in words. Their experience of God doesn't always need words. On several occasions in the gospels Jesus used children as an illustration of those to whom the Kingdom of God belonged encouraging adults to 'become as a child' in order to enter that kingdom (Luke 18:15–17; Mark 10:13–16; Matthew 19:13–15).

Many adults' lives have been greatly influenced by the faith of a child. By sharing in their experiences, teaching them appropriately, guiding them gently, and enabling them to grow in body, mind and spirit they too have come to a greater understanding of God, his relationship with us and plan and purpose for our lives. We live in an age where two, almost three generations of adults have had little or no positive teaching about God or experience of the church. Many of these are the parents of the children in our pre-school groups. Some of us reading these introductory pages (including the writer!) will not have received a Sunday school education but others will have been nurtured in the Christian faith from the cradle. Many of the stories we share with our children will be new to us. The action rhymes and songs of praise may be the first 'hymns' we have ever sung. Many of the ideas for prayer will be our introduction to prayer. It's a whole new journey, one in which our children will undoubtedly lead us, but a journey which, in hindsight, we shall all travel together.

Why share spiritual truths with young children? Because we all want the very best for our children and in seeking to provide the best we are all privileged to learn from them in the process.

Where and when?

Where and when you use *Tiddlywinks* material will vary considerably, as will the extent of the use of the material provided. Each session incorporates different child-centred activities linked by a theme: play time; game time; making time; story time; rhyme time; song time; pray time. You may be in a position to influence everything that happens in your group and therefore, make use of any number of these. Alternatively you may have responsibility for one part of your group's programme, eg the singing time, a craft activity, or story time. The joy of *Tiddlywinks* is that you can simply extract what you need for use at any one time.

Let's look at the variety of different contexts in which pre-school groups meet and the way in which they might use *Tiddlywinks* material:

Midweek 'Pram' Services:

Tiddlywinks contains all that a leader might need for these short, midweek 'services' of worship for pre-school children. Time may prevent them from using all the material and lack of suitable facilities may restrict the type of playtime and making time, especially if these groups meet inside the main body of their church (although there are a number of ingenious and creative ways of adapting what might at first seem insurmountable obstacles). But, provided they have an area in which they can move safely and sit comfortably together, game, story, pray, rhyme and song time will be ideal for these occasions.

Midweek Parent/Carer and Toddler Groups:

These important groups provide a much needed meeting point in the community particularly for first time parents and carers of young children. They are led by a wide range of people, including leaders formally appointed by the church, Christian mums who attend the group with their own children, and mums, or carers, who have little contact with the church but who use (often renting) church buildings as a meeting place. Some will run along very similar lines to pram services seeking to provide a place where Christian values will be experienced and the faith taught. Others, will simply be seeking to provide quality play and creative stimulation for the children present. *Tiddlywinks* material can meet both of these needs with leaders carefully selecting what they feel is appropriate for their situation. Whilst each section is thematically linked it can also stand on its own. Linking a five-minute craft activity with a ten-minute singing time may be all that is required whilst others will incorporate a story and prayer time. It is totally flexible.

Sunday groups

Many Sunday crèches and early years teaching groups (usually for children aged two-and-a-half to five years) will be looking for a balanced teaching programme to follow over a set number of different weeks, covering the whole of the church's festivals and seasons. These children will generally come from Christian homes and families where the faith is lived as well as taught. *Tiddlywinks* will offer an extensive range of topics and themes ideally suited to this context, and of course the teaching and learning style is always child-centred and age appropriate.

Playgroups and Nurseries

Most playgroups and nurseries for two-and-a-half to five-year-olds are officially registered with OFSTED and seek to follow the early years educational goals and guidelines. Leaders are trained and fully responsible for the children in their care. Whilst not written with the sole intention of meeting the educational requirements of these goals, much of the material will serve to enhance and supplement the curriculum required for these groups.

Informal settings, eg coffee mornings and drop-in centres

These informal and casual places of meeting provided by many churches regularly attract young children but rarely provide adequate facilities for them. Following five minutes of biscuit munching they are bored and restless. A simple craft activity, a couple of songs and rhymes, and short story can make their short visit a very valuable experience. It's a statement about how much we value these children as well as a valuable teaching opportunity. It also encourages them to return.

Special events

Many churches recognise that what happens on a Sunday morning is often inaccessible and inappropriate to young children and their families. But this does not always mean that there is not an interest in learning about and experiencing the Christian faith. Many groups are experimenting with occasional events geared entirely for young families at a time that is suitable for them. Some have found Saturday tea times a good meeting time, others Sunday afternoons. Festivals, ie Christmas, Easter, Harvest etc are excellent starting points for these and often draw large numbers of people, especially when food is part of the programme. The *Tiddlywinks* special feature (designed for big group events – see pages 90 and 91 and/or *Tiddlywinks* session material can be creatively used to provide a theme base with all the necessary ingredients for an enjoyable family-friendly programme.

How?

How?

When setting out to run a group for pre-school children and their carers there are practical things to consider which are essential, others that are recommended and others still that are a bonus. This page outlines all three. It also includes a recommended plan of action for any who might be starting from scratch.

ESSENTIAL

Health and safety

Imagine the building to be used for the group as your own home and apply the same levels of health and safety requirements. Check heaters, floor surfaces, furniture, plug sockets, secure entry and exit points, fire exits, toilet and baby changing facilities, kitchen hygiene and safety if serving refreshments. Be aware of the different allergies that could affect children and encourage leaders to attend a First Aid course. Aim for the highest possible standards of health and safety at all times.

Child Protection

In the UK, The 1989 Children's Act is designed to encourage good practice and safety in all work undertaken with children aged 0–18 years of age, including that in churches. Any church-sponsored group where children remain in the care of leaders for longer than two hours, and which meets more than six times a year, is required to register with the Social Services department of the local authority. Many of our playgroups and nurseries fall into this category, but parent and toddler groups do not need to register, although many choose to notify local authorities of their existence. Where parents and carers remain with their children for the duration of the session they are held responsible for their own children. Each church denomination or network has drawn up its own guidelines for good practice with recommendations for group leaders working in this context. These can be obtained from national headquarters or through regional children's advisors and should be followed carefully in order to maintain the highest of standards possible.

If you are working outside the UK, please check up on the Child Protection legislation for your area.

Insurance cover

Insurance for pre-school groups should have appropriate and adequate cover. Existing church policies should always be checked. Specialist agencies such as the *Pre-School Learning Alliance* or *Playgroup Network* work with major insurance companies to provide tailor-made packages for pre-school groups.

RECOMMENDED

Storage facilities

You can never have enough storage! What might start as one plastic box full of toys and materials will quickly multiply. Borrow, beg, plead and cry for more boxes, shelves, cupboards, and storerooms that are easily accessible, make setting out and clearing away as easy as possible

Keeping records

The fire service require a written record of all persons in a public building at any time which provides a very useful record of all who have attended. Additional information such as addresses, phone numbers, birth dates help to inform members in the event of unexpected group closure due to bad weather or sickness, and to acknowledge birthdays of children, all of which shows care and concern. Ensure, however, that confidentiality is maintained with all personal details kept on file. In accordance with the Data Protection Act, do not divulge any information to third parties.

A photocopiable registration form can be found on the inside front cover of *Tiddlywinks: The Big Red Book*.

Teamwork

This work requires storytellers, singers, craft specialists, people who will keep a register, take monies, make refreshments, set out and clear away, etc. Where teamwork is fostered it also becomes a training ground for future leaders: those making coffee may develop into wonderful storytellers, songwriters or craft workers. Try to create an atmosphere where people are free to learn and you will grow your own leaders naturally.

Budgeting

Much of this work incorporates both the spiritual nurture of children and outreach to carers and families. Many churches allocate a specific amount of budget money for this purpose but don't always recognise the context in which it is being done. Be sure to remind them and ask for ongoing financial support to fund the work. Training leaders, publicity, resource books, craft materials, play equipment, refreshments and various other miscellaneous items can be costly. Keep a record of expenditure and income, with proof of purchases at all times. Don't be worried about making a charge for the group, as many parents/carers are more than willing to contribute towards something that their children enjoy.

BONUS

Behind the scene helpers

There are many housebound people in our churches who love to be involved in children's work. Publicity, programmes and newsletters can be designed on computers; craft materials cut and prepared well in advance and prayer can be a vital and encouraging support to a tired and weary leader. A little advance planning can alleviate a lot of pressure when shared with willing home-based workers.

Outside funding

Occasionally groups have benefited from charitable grants. Different bodies vary considerably in the criteria set out for funding – many decline groups that promote religious activities whilst others seem much more open. Local libraries usually have details of local and national charities.

If starting your group from scratch you should always seek the permission and support of your church leadership body. Go equipped with a well thought through plan of action.

Playing with a purpose

Play is the basis for almost every part of the *Tiddlywinks* material because the writers know and understand that young children learn everything through playing. Their capacity to listen is limited to just one minute for each year of life and so the suggestions offered include very few 'listening only' activities. In recent years educationalists have confirmed that all ages of children and adults learn far more through what they do and experience than simply through what they hear.

Each part of the theme-based *Tiddlywinks* programme is designed to offer young children some kind of play with a purpose. As a child moves from one activity to another, joining in small and large group experiences, he or she is gathering understanding and experience of that topic or theme. Of course some won't make the connections, but others will.

What is most important is that each activity is accessible and meaningful and it is the leader's task to provide the basic ingredients and stimulus for creating the best possible, purposeful play experience. Let's consider the different play sections of the programme:

Play time

(unstructured play)
'Play time' describes a variety of unstructured play activities, many of which will connect with children's every day life and experiences. This is likely to take up the bulk of the session and greet children on arrival. It will help introduce them to the day's topic, eg animals for story of Noah, boats for story of Jesus and the storm, food for story of feeding 5,000 etc, acquire the vocabulary (when stimulated by adults) for use in the songs and rhymes, and explore concepts, eg animal families, effects of water, sharing out food between friends and dolls. All these play experiences are valuable in their own right but also become important foundations in a programme designed to help young children learn about a specific Christian story or Bible truth.

Game time

(cooperative play)
Young children generally play alone but simple, non-competitive games will develop an awareness of others and a sense of belonging to a group. They will learn to share, take turns, watch (and imitate) others, express delight in both their own and others' achievements, and respond to each other. Physically active games also stimulate physical development especially coordination and balance. Games can strengthen relationships within a group and help create a community built on Christian values, as well as provide a greater understanding and experience of the story or theme being developed.

Story time

(engaging play)
When creatively led, a story time demands much more than just listening. Most Bible stories lend themselves to visual, sound and action aids, actively engaging as many of the children's senses as you possibly can. Participation will involve ears, voices, hands (and legs) but also the emotions. Young children will live through the characters they are introduced to, imagining, feeling, sensing, and exploring all aspects of the story you are telling. They may not be able to respond with words but they will be learning.

Making time

(creative play)
Creative play introduces young children to a whole new world. The learning here most definitely takes place in the process of making and not in the end product, even though it will be greatly cherished and a very important reminder of the day's theme or story. Size, shape, texture, colour and patterns are just some of the important discoveries that will be made through making. Children will explore a variety of materials and acquire new skills and techniques. Together parents, carers and children will grow in confidence and creativity; they will uncover the mark of a creative God within them, in whose image they have been made. Whatever the limitations on your space and facilities make 'Making time' possible, as it is one of the most valuable learning experiences of all.

Song time and Rhyme time

(musical play)
Music, rhythm, rhyme and movement are experiences of the womb so it's not surprising that even the youngest of babes will actively respond to this part of the programme. When part of a circle time the learning is far more than simply the words of songs and rhymes being used. Young children learn to listen, follow actions, take turns, recognise each other and be part of a group experience. Even those who appear not to be participating amaze parents by repeating everything they have learnt hours later when at home!

Adults too

Never underestimate all that adults are learning through the children's play programme. Some are actually learning how to play themselves; others are learning Bible stories and truths for the first time; and others will want to develop that learning through further adult-centred programmes. *Tiddlywinks* even provides suggestions for ways in which you might help them to do so.

Making the most of structure

Under-fives love routine and structure. They learn through rhythm and repetition. It makes them feel secure and safe and helps them to quickly identify people, situations and experiences. As these become positive experiences children will look for them, ask for them and sometime be very difficult to handle when they don't get them!

Structure doesn't mean boring repetition or inflexibility. It is determined by the basic needs of the children in our care. Every child needs to eat (even if they don't want to!) and so the structure of our day includes several eating times, but, exactly when, where and what we eat is determined by the individual's needs and circumstances. In the same way, a group including young children and their carers needs to have a structure that has been fashioned and shaped to meet the needs and circumstances of its members.

Tiddlywinks material is shaped into a structure that incorporates several important components; 'Welcome' time; 'Circle' time and 'Home' time. Each are created to produce familiarity and security for both carers and children.

Welcome time
Providing a welcome is all about creating a sense of belonging, being part of a community. The key to doing it lies in being ready. Try out the ideas on pages 92 and 93.

Ready for children
The room or area being used should act like a magnet to every child so that they are immediately drawn into a play activity of some kind. Pre-schoolers are not able to sit around waiting for everyone to arrive! They need to play. When setting out your room make safe provision for babies and early toddlers, keep large pieces of equipment and mobile toys away from activity tables and encourage adult participation by positioning chairs close to activity tables.

Ready for adults
Establishing eye contact and welcoming individuals by name are the two most important acts of welcome. A one-to-one personal approach helps adults feel they and their children belong to a caring community. It reflects the love and care that Christians know God has for each individual.

Ready for newcomers
Newcomers need special treatment. First experiences are lasting ones and once put off they rarely give you a second chance. A leader should be allocated specifically to the task of welcoming new adults and children. Often there are details that need to be taken and procedures to explain which take time. It can also be helpful to provide a little leaflet describing the group, its purpose and structure, giving useful contact numbers.

Tiddlywinks provides a number of suggestions for activities that help build a sense of welcome. Remember whatever you choose it will necessitate you being ready – the most important welcome factor of them all!

Circle Time
Circle time is all about communication, for which you will need to be prepared. It's about preparing any number of the story, rhyme, song and prayer activities suggested in the *Tiddlywinks* material to engage both children and adults within a simple circle. The 'circle' shape is important as it includes everyone and brings them into a position where they can see and join in with what is happening. Participation by everyone is crucial to the success of circle time and many groups choose to go into a separate area or room to avoid distractions of toys and equipment; others simply clear away before starting. This time is key to developing the sense of belonging and group ownership from which will grow shared responsibility and strong community ties.

When you are part of a community you share special occasions together. It may be a birthday (adult's or child's!), special anniversary (of the group or church) or celebration of a newborn baby. Circle time is the ideal time to focus on these special occasions. There may also be sad times for which the group as a whole need to find an expression of shock, grief or sorrow, eg bereavement of a child, a national tragedy, a local concern. The simple lighting of a candle, a song or prayer may be sensitively incorporated into this special time together.

Home time
So far, creating our structure has involved being ready and being prepared. Ensuring a positive home time means we have to be organised. Too often under-fives groups simply disintegrate with no positive means of finishing or saying goodbye. People drift away as leaders scurry around tidying up. A positive ending gives a feeling of satisfaction and completion and develops a sense of anticipation for the next meeting.

Many group sessions end with a circle time building in a final song or rhyme that indicates 'this is the end'. *Tiddlywinks* offers a number of different ways in which you can mark the end in this way. Look at the ideas on pages 94 and 95 and try to choose one that best suits your group, and let it become part of your routine.

Quick tips to get you started...

Many experienced children's leaders find working with groups of young children daunting, especially when parents and carers are present. The skills and confidence required are quite different to those needed to work with older children. If you are new to this age range, or it has been some years since you've had contact with them, spend some time simply being with them and familiarising yourself with their behaviour and play patterns. You will be amazed at how quickly you acquire the knowledge and experience necessary for leading various parts of the *Tiddlywinks* programme. Here are a few tips to get you started:

● Using the Bible with young children

Do explain that the Bible is God's very special storybook

Do show the children a child-friendly Bible each time you tell a Bible story so that they become familiar with it

Do make it accessible to them and encourage them to borrow a copy to take home

Don't read straight from the Bible, always 'tell' a story

Do communicate an enthusiasm and excitement for the stories you tell, remembering that you share God's story

Do be prepared for the many questions that some children will ask!

● Storytelling

Do make it short (remember one minute of attention for each year of a child's life)

Do sit where you can see and be seen

Do make it visual, eg large pictures, household objects, puppets, *Duplo*, or toys

Do involve the children in actions, sounds, and repetitive phrases

Do give them time and space to respond to the stories with their comments and questions

Don't be worried about repeating the story, especially if they have enjoyed it!

● Leading songs and rhymes

Don't worry about not being able to play an instrument

Do sit at the children's level when leading

Don't teach more than one new song at any one time

Don't pitch songs and rhymes too high or use complex tunes

Do use children's instruments but,

Don't forget to put them away afterwards

Do encourage parents and carers to join in

Do use familiar tunes and write your own words

● Behaviour

Do make sure that parents and carers know they are responsible for their children

Do offer support to a parent/carer whose child is going through a difficult stage

Don't discuss the behaviour of their child in front of others

Do remember there is nearly always a reason for bad behaviour, eg boredom, neglect, inappropriate play, tiredness, hunger etc

Do develop positive strategies for dealing with common behaviour patterns in young children, eg biting, pushing, unwillingness to share, tantrums, dirty nappy!

Do encourage parents and carers to deal with difficult behaviour and

Don't intervene unless a child is in danger

● Craft

Do protect tables, floors and children if using messy materials

Do supervise at all times

Do let the children do the activity! (Provide additional materials if adults want a go.)

Don't worry too much about the end product

Do have hand-washing facilities ready

Don't allow the activity to go on too long

Do create drying space for activities needing to dry

Do be sure to put the child's name on the activity at the start

Do allow children to take them home – make more if you need a display

Do make the most of creating displays – it is a presence of the group in their absence

● Prayer

Do make prayers short, simple and spontaneous

Do try using a candle, bell or simple prayer song to introduce a prayer time

Do encourage different kinds of prayer, eg 'thank you', 'sorry' and 'please' prayers

Don't always insist on hands together, eyes closed

Do encourage action, rhyme and song prayers

Don't miss the opportunity to send written prayers into the home through craft activities

Do consider writing your own special prayer for the group that the children can learn and grow familiar with

● Involving parents and carers

Do spend time fostering good friendships with parents and carers

Do make clear to them that they are responsible for their children

Do encourage maximum participation at all times

Don't expect a parent/carer with more than one child to carry responsibility for activities

Do look out for hidden talents and leadership skills

Don't reject genuine offers of help and support

Do affirm, support and encourage parents and carers at all times.

Working with young children is hard work but we gain far more than we ever give. Be warned – shopping in your local supermarket will never be the same again. You will be gurgled at, sung to, waved at and clearly shouted at from one end of the freezers to the other. Entering the world of young children in your community will provide you with a whole new family! And together you will become part of God's family.

Additional resources
to help and support you in your work with young children and their parents/carers.

Recommended Children's Bibles and storybooks

The Beginners Bible (Zondervan)

The Lion First Bible (Lion Publishing)

Lift the Flap Bible (Candle Books)

Me Too! Books, Marilyn Lashbrook (Candle Books) 16 different titles with interactive stories from both the New and Old Testament

Tiddlywinks: My Little Red Book – First Steps in Bible Reading, Ro Willoughby (Scripture Union)

Tiddlywinks: My Little Blue Book – First Steps in Bible Reading, Penny Boshoff (Scripture Union)

Action Rhyme series, Stephanie Jeffs (Scripture Union) 4 titles:
Come into the Ark with Noah; March Round the Walls with Joshua; Follow the Star with the Wise Men; Share out the Food with Jesus

Bible Concertina books, Nicola Edwards and Kate Davies (Scripture Union)
The Creation; Noah's Ark; The Christmas Baby

The Bible Pebbles series, Tim and Jenny Wood (Scripture Union)

Daniel in the Lion's Den; Jonah and the Big Fish; Moses in the Basket; Noah's Ark; The First Christmas; The First Easter; Jesus the Healer; Jesus the Teacher

The Little Fish series, Gordon Stowell (Scripture Union)

Lots of titles about Jesus, other Bible people, and you and me.

Jigsaw Bible activity books 2, 3 and 4 (Scripture Union)

Things Jesus Did, Stories Jesus Told, People Jesus Met, Baby Jesus, Stephanie Jeffs (Bible Reading Fellowship)

Prayer Books

Pray and Play: 101 Creative prayer ideas for use with under-fives, Kathy L Cannon (Scripture Union)

The Pick a Prayer Series, Tim and Jenny Wood, illustrated by Suzy-Jane Tanner (Scripture Union), 4 spiral-bound board titles:

Pick-a-prayer: For Bedtime; Pick-a-prayer: For Every Day; Pick-a-prayer: For Special Days; Pick-a-prayer: To Say Thank You

My Little Prayer Box, (Scripture Union)

Hello God, it's me, Stephanie King and Helen Mahood (Scripture Union)

The Lion Book of First Prayers, Sue Box (Lion Publishing)

What Shall We Pray About? Andy Robb (Candle)

Prayers with the Bears (John Hunt Publishing) 4 titles

101 Ideas for Creative Prayer, New Ideas for Creative Prayer, Judith Merrell (Scripture Union)

Song/Rhyme Books

Let's Sing and Shout! ed. Maggie Barfield (Scripture Union)

Let's All Clap Hands! ed. Maggie Barfield (Scripture Union)

Jump Up If You're Wearing Red (NS/CHP)

Feeling Good!, Peter Churchill (NS/CHP)

Bobby Shaftoe, clap your hands, Sue Nicholls, (A&C Black) Includes 37 familiar and traditional tunes with simple guitar chords)

Kidsource Books 1 and 2 (Kevin Mayhew). A general selection for children, including many suitable for under-fives.

Other resources

God and Me series, exploring emotions and Christian beliefs (Scripture Union):
Really, really scared; Really, really excited; I love you; I miss you, Leena Lane
What's heaven like?; What's God like?; What's in the Bible?; Can Jesus hear me? Stephanie King

Resources to support parents and carers

Lion Pocketbook Series, various authors (Lion Publishing) Over 15 different titles on both faith-searching issues, eg *Why Believe?; Why Pray?*, and pastoral issues, eg *Why Marry?; When a child dies*. These are inexpensive pocketbooks ideal for use with parents and carers.

First Steps Video for parents inquiring about infant baptism, (CPAS)

Welcome to Baptism, Journey of a Lifetime Video, Grayswood Studio

Time out for Parents, Positive Parenting Publications, First Floor, 2A South Street, Gosport PO12 1ES. A comprehensive teaching pack, covering most aspects of parenting from infancy to teenage years

Just a minute: Biblical reflections for busy mums, Christine Orme (Scripture Union)

Family Caring Trust
Director: Michael Quinn, 44 Rathfriland Rd, Newry, Co. Down, N Ireland BT34 1LD
The Family Caring Trust produce an extensive range of parenting courses focusing on different age ranges of children. These have been widely used and appreciated in pre-school community groups.

CARE for the Family P.O. Box 448
Cardiff CF15 7YY
CARE produce a wide range of resources to support parents including a video based course called Parent Talk, books, training and special parent and child weekends.

Courses for parents/carers who wish to explore questions and issues of faith:

Emmaus, National Society

Alpha, Holy Trinity Brompton

Additional Leaders Resource Material

SALT 3-4+ for leaders and *Sparklers* activity material for children (Scripture Union)

Tiddlywinks: The Big Red and Blue Books/My Little Red and Blue Books (Scripture Union)

Glitter and Glue: 101 creative craft ideas for use with under-fives, Annette Oliver (Scripture Union)

Praise Play and Paint, Jan Godfrey (NS/CHP)

Under Fives Alive and *Under Fives – Alive and Kicking*, Farley, Goddard, Jarvis, (NS/CHP)

Bible Fun for the Very Young, Vicki Howe (Bible Reading Fellowship)

Bible Stuff, Janet Gaukroger (CPAS) 5 titles in the series.

The following 2 titles are packed with ideas for encouraging parents and children to celebrate the Christian year at home:
Feast of Faith, Kevin and Stephanie Parkes (NS/CHP)
The 'E' Book, Gill Ambrose (NS/CHP)

Background Reading

Working with Under 6s, Val Mullally (Scripture Union)

Children Finding Faith, Francis Bridger (Scripture Union/CPAS)

Bringing Children to Faith, Penny Frank (Scripture Union/CPAS)

Children and the Gospel, Ron Buckland (Scripture Union)

The Adventure Begins, Terry Clutterham (Scripture Union/CPAS)

Seen and Heard, Jackie Cray (Monarch)

Sharing Jesus with Under Fives, Janet Gaukroger (Crossway Books)

Networks and Organisations supporting work with young children

Pre-school Learning Alliance
61-63 Kings Cross Rd, London WC1X9LL

Playgroup Network, PO Box 23, Whitely Bay, Tyne and Wear, NE26 3DB

Scripture Union
207-209 Queensway, Bletchley, Milton Keynes, MK2 2EB. www.scriptureunion.org.uk
For readers in other countries, please contact your national Scripture Union office for details.

The Mothers' Union
23 Tufton, St London SW1P3RB

Church Pastoral Aid Society
Jackie Cray, Advisor for Families and Under-fives, Athena Drive, Tachbrook Park, WARWICK CV34 6NG

Playleader – an ecumenical magazine linking Christians working with Under-fives
The Editor, Diana Turner, 125 Finchfield Lane, Wolverhampton WV3 8EY

How to plan your group programme using Tiddlywinks

Tiddlywinks Big Books provide resources, ideas and activities for use in any pre-school setting. Whether you are running a carer and toddler group; a playgroup or pre-school; a nursery or nursery school; a child-minding network; a crèche or toddler club; a conventional Sunday morning group at church; a drop-in centre, a coffee morning or a pram service – or any other place or group where under-fives gather together; *Tiddlywinks* has suggestions to help you.

Here, some pre-school practitioners choose their own options from the outlines in this book for their own different types of group, using the topic 'I can see' on page 14.

Priscilla is a playgroup supervisor, running a group for 20 children, three sessions a week. And once a month, she also leads a pram service (20 minutes with refreshments and craft activity afterwards) for young children and 'their' adults.

Priscilla's choice

For pram service

Story time: 'a good simple story with visual impact'

Song time: 'we would use two or three of these songs'

Pray time: 'simple – and with children involved'

After the service we would use Play time: Cut and stick or the Making time: Binoculars or Masks. The Activity page: either during the craft time or to take away.

Fey has been leading Mites and Minders, a carer and toddler group, for seven years. Fey says, 'Mites and Minders meets in the church hall. Its aim is two-fold, to provide a service to children and adults, and as a stepping stone towards faith. Specifically Christian activities are very low key. We promote relevant church activities and enjoy an occasional child-free evening together.'

Fey's choice

'I would use "I can see" for two weeks and if it went well, would have a third session.'

Play time: Look and see and Cut and stick.

Game time: Guess who? and Feely bag

Making time: Binoculars

Story time: Jesus heals a blind man (the other activities will have set the scene so the children will understand the Christian emphasis of this activity)

Song time: adapting 'Thank you God for this fine day' and 'A sailor went to sea'

Adults too: a video and popcorn evening

Activity page: Masks 'I would photocopy them on to card, so you don't have to do the sticking at home.'

Angie works as a nursery nurse at a busy day nursery during the week and also runs a church crèche for babies and very young children on Sunday mornings.

Angie's choices

For nursery

The nursery is multicultural and multi-faith so it would not always be appropriate to use a Bible story or certain activities. And the nursery day is very structured and organised so any activities have to fit the nursery timings, not the other way round!

Play time: some good ideas here which would fit in well with the nursery free play sessions. The Cut and stick is easy to prepare and easy for the children to do themselves, with little help.

Game time: the Feely bag idea could be used with all the children, just after our afternoon registration, while they are all together.

Making time: masks are always popular with our children; I'd use this as a main activity in our Art session, with the collage as a secondary activity.

Story time: I'd read this after morning registration when the children are most awake and receptive and then recap it after afternoon registration time.

Rhyme time: the children will love making up their own actions and joining in with this.

Song time: our children enjoy singing so I'd use most of these songs – and any others I could think of which fitted the theme!

For crèche

Angie says, 'Very few of the children are old enough for any activities and space is limited for active games or craft. As they get older, we prepare them to move on to a more structured group with a maximum half hour session, like this:

Story (5 minutes, very simple, using pictures as visual aids); Song (a very simple 'Thank you God for eyes to see' repeated several times); Game (5 minutes using the Feely bag option); Free play (10 minutes or so, using the Cut and stick suggestion which younger ones can join too); and ending with Pray time. It's good to get children into prayer early. I would use their collages and say, 'I can see...' with them joining in 'Thank you God for eyes to see.'

I would use the activity page as a take-home leaflet so that the children have something to share with their parents and to initiate conversations about what they have done in their group.'

B1 All about me
I can see

Jesus heals a blind man

John 9:1–34

Play time

You will need: interesting things for the children to look at (or look through), eyes cut from newspapers and magazines, glue sticks, paper, camcorder and television.

Look and see

Have a selection of free-play activities set out for when the children first arrive. Include one special table with a display of things that are interesting to look at or look through – for example, toy telescopes, binoculars, magnifying glasses, sunglasses, prisms, 3D glasses and books, picture-books, pop-up and lift-the-flap books, photos, kaleidoscopes, child-safe mirrors. Encourage all the children to visit this table for a couple of minutes at some point and ask a leader to be there to chat with the children.

Cut and stick

On another table, have a selection of eyes cut from papers and magazines for the children to glue, collage-style, onto a sheet of paper.
Although this activity might seem pointless to an adult, children love gluing and sticking, and it helps to develop their hand-eye coordination. Add the child's name and the caption: 'Thank you God for eyes to see!' at the top of each collage. While they are working, take the opportunity to talk about eyes and all the things that they help us to do.

On camera

Finally, if your meeting-room boasts a television and someone in your group owns a camcorder, why not film the children while they play, chat, sing and make things? Show the film, which should be no more than 8–10 minutes long, later in the session, so that the children can see themselves on screen. Children love to watch themselves on video, and this kind of activity can aid their emotional development by helping them to form a concept of their own identity. Comment on the fact that our eyes help us to see all kinds of exciting things; we can even see ourselves on television.

no limit

Game time

You will need: blindfold, one or more feely bags with 6–8 items inside.

Guess who?

Ask a leader to wear a blindfold and guess the identity of five or six children and carers by using their senses of hearing and touch. Then, allow any children who want to wear the blindfold to do the same. Don't let this activity run on too long; three or four minutes is ample. You can always return to it later if it proves popular.

Feely bag

In advance, prepare a special feely bag – a pillowcase secured at the top will work well. Place inside 6–8 items that the children can guess by their shape and size. Put the bag in the middle of your group and let everyone take a turn to guess an object. With a larger group, you might want to prepare more than one bag. Explain that people whose eyes don't work properly have to use their hands and ears to help them identify people and objects. Today, we are going to hear a story about someone who couldn't see at all.

3-5 mins per game

Making time

You will need: one copy of the activity page per child, thin card, glue sticks, scissors, wooden drinks stirrers or strips of card, sticky tape.

Making masks

Make a copy of the mask on this week's activity page for each child to decorate with crayons, glitter or sticky shapes. Parents or carers can then help the children to glue the mask onto thin card and cut it out. Fix a wooden drinks stirrer or length of thick card to the back of the mask with sticky tape, so that it can be held up in front of the eyes.

Binoculars

For an alternative craft activity, make binoculars out of cardboard kitchen rolls. Cut the kitchen roll in half, glue or tape the two sides together and add a length of wool to make a strap. Decorate the binoculars with sticky shapes.

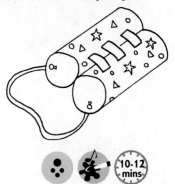

10-12 mins

Story time

You will need: eight very simple pictures, as described below.

Draw eight very simple pictures to show the children as you tell the story (see illustration). The first picture of Tim (1) shows him with closed eyes and a sad mouth. Simply add three or four extra lines, as the children watch, to achieve picture 9.

Once there was a man who was very sad. The Bible doesn't tell us what his name was, so I'm going to call him Tim (1). Tim was very sad because he couldn't see. He couldn't see the sun in the daytime (2) or the moon at night (3). He couldn't see the smiley faces of his friends (4). He couldn't see green trees (5) and colourful flowers (6). He couldn't see his own fingers (7) or his own toes (8). Tim didn't even know what his own family looked like.

One day, Tim heard lots of people coming his way. 'I wonder what's happening!' he thought to himself.

Then he heard a kind voice. 'Don't worry!' said the voice. 'My name is Jesus, and I'm going to help you.' Quickly, Jesus made some mud. Then, very gently, he put the mud on Tim's eyes. (**Health and safety note:** make sure that the children understand that ordinarily you should never put mud in your eyes!)

'Yuck!' thought Tim. 'That feels horrible!'

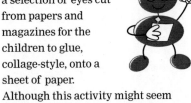

'Now then,' said Jesus, 'I want you to go and wash off the mud in Siloam Pool.'

Tim carefully washed off the mud in the cool, clear water, and when he'd finished he was amazed and delighted *(1)*.

First, Tim saw the light dancing on the water. Then, he looked down and he could see his own toes peeping out of his sandals *(8)* and his own fingers dripping with water *(7)*. He looked around and he could see the beautiful coloured flowers *(6)* and the tall, green trees *(5)*. Then he saw the smiling faces of his friends *(4)*, and when he looked up he could see the sun in the sky *(2)*. All of these things were quite new to Tim, so he was very happy and excited.

Soon, some of Tim's neighbours came to see what all the fuss was about. At first, they didn't recognise him because he was so happy and his eyes were wide with excitement. 'What's happened? How can you see?' they all asked.

'It was a man called Jesus,' said Tim. 'He healed my eyes so that I can see. Jesus is amazing. I must find him and thank him.'

Rhyme time

Repeat this rhyme two or three times. Make up actions together.

I can see the sun in the morning;
　　I can see the stars at night.
I can't see anything in the dark;
　　I can see everything when it's light.
I can see all the children;

I can see the grown-ups, too
I can see the colour of your eyes –
　　they're brown and green and blue.
I can see films and videos
　　and my favourite TV shows;
I can see ten wiggly fingers;
　　I can even see my nose!
There are so many things
　　that my eyes can see;
I'm so glad that God gave my eyes to me.

Song time

You will need: music for the songs listed below.

Adapt 'Thank you God for this fine day' *JP* 232 to 'Thank you God for eyes to see (x3) ... all the things you made.'
'Two little eyes to look to God' *SKS 345 (This could be used as a series song.)*
'He gave me eyes so I could see' *JP* 74. *(This would also work as a series song.)*
'A sailor went to sea, sea, sea, to see what he could see, see, see, but all that he could see, see, see was the bottom of the deep blue sea, sea, sea.' *(Traditional.)*

Pray time

Practise the response to this prayer. Then lead the children in at the end of each couplet.

My eyes see colours:
　　red, yellow, green and blue.
My eyes see people,
　　friends and family, me and you.
So I say... *Thank you, God, for eyes that see!*

My eyes see flowers
　　and green, leafy trees.
My eyes see rivers
　　and sparkling seas.
So I say... *Thank you, God, for eyes that see!*

My eyes see winks
　　and smiles and friendly faces.
My eyes see shops and houses,
　　thousands of places.
So I say... *Thank you, God, for eyes that see!*

My eyes see pictures and photos
　　and pages of writing.
There are so many things
　　for my eyes to delight in.
So I say... *Thank you, God, for eyes that see!*

Extra time

•Read *Elmer's Colours*, by David McKee (Andersen Press Ltd. ISBN 0-86264-493-3).

•Make mosaic patterns out of coloured stickers.

•Find out how many children have blue, green or brown eyes, and make a chart.

•Help children to tear out beautiful scenes from travel brochures to make a collage with the heading: 'Thank you, God, that I can see the beauty of your world.'

•Take photos of the children at work and play and develop them so that they can see them next week.

Adults too

A visual treat! Is there a suitable film on at the cinema this week? If not, why not have a video evening at someone's home, with an interval for pizza and popcorn? Take the opportunity to meet the parents or carers in a different environment, away from the pressures of child care.

Top tip

What do people see as they first walk into your room? Is there a welcoming display, or something visually exciting? Why not take some group photos and put them on the wall? You could also include photos of other church activities to encourage new mums to come along. Have a pile of church magazines available and pin up current news-sheets so that visitors can see that there is more on offer, besides the *Tiddlywinks* group.

ACTIVITY PAGE: Photocopy the artwork on page 18 directly onto thin card for use

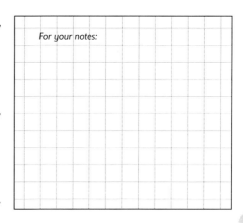

For your notes:

B2 All about me
I can talk
Philip and the Ethiopian

Acts 8: 26–40

Play time

You will need: toy telephones, tape recorder, magazine pictures, round-ended scissors, sticky labels, small boxes, crayons, cardboard tubes.

Time to talk
Have a selection of free-play activities set out for when the children first arrive and, since this week is all about talking, have one or two toy telephones, walkie-talkies and play microphones available.

Make a phone
On one table have a selection of small boxes, paper, crayons and sticky labels ready for junk-modelling. Encourage the youngsters to make pretend telephones or mobile phones. Cover a small rectangular box with coloured paper. Then write the numbers 0–9 on sticky labels and stick them onto the top of the box. Add two small labels to represent the speaking and receiving holes. If you're making mobile phones, don't forget to add a strip of card for an aerial.

Make a microphone
Colour in cardboard tubes and fix a scrunched-up ball of paper to one end.

Cut and snip
On another table have ready some round-ended scissors and a selection of old magazines. Encourage the children to cut out lots of pictures of mouths and talking heads. These can be put aside to use during the prayer time.

Mini interviews
Ask a leader to act as a roving reporter and walk round with a tape recorder, asking the youngsters a couple of simple questions. Record their answers to play back later, so that the children can listen to the sound of their own voices.

no limit

Game time

You will need: toy phone or mobile phone.

Who am I calling?
Explain to your group that you have one or two telephone calls to make and perhaps they'd like to listen in. Maybe they can guess whom you are talking to.

A. My hair's a little long. I wonder if you could fit me in one afternoon this week? Thursday at two o'clock… that would be great.

B. Can you tell me what time the train leaves for Bristol? And how long does the journey take? How much will a return ticket cost?

C. My little boy has had a bad cough for over a week. Can I have an appointment this morning?

5 mins

Making time

You will need: an empty plastic milk bottle for each child, sticky shapes.

Megaphones

Collect a number of clean plastic milk bottles (the kind that have handles). Discard the lids and cut off the bottom of the bottles, so that you are left with a superb megaphone shape, complete with its own handle (see illustration). Help the children to decorate their megaphones with sticky shapes. When the whole group has finished, encourage them to march round the room with their megaphones, chanting something suitably rousing! For example:

We are the *Tiddlywinks* group marching up and down
And when we use our megaphones we're heard all over town!

5 mins

Story time

The following story highlights the fact that Philip loved to talk about Jesus. Show the children how to open and shut their fingers and thumb to make their hand resemble a chattering mouth. Explain that you want them to join in the story by saying: *'Chatter, chatter, chatter!' and by opening and shutting their fingers whenever they see you doing the same.*

Philip loved to chat to people (*chatter, chatter, chatter*). He loved to chat to them about Jesus and about how much God loved them (*chatter, chatter, chatter*). One day, Philip was walking along a lonely road. He knew that God had a job for him. 'I wonder what God wants me to do here,' he thought to himself. 'I can't see anyone to chat to.' (*Chatter, chatter, chatter.*) At that moment, an important Ethiopian official was coming along the road in his chariot. It was a beautiful chariot, with bright painted wheels, pulled by a handsome horse. The official was a tall, dark-skinned man with a worried face. He was very busy reading a book. 'I wonder if God wants me to chat to this man,' thought Philip (*chatter, chatter, chatter*). As the chariot went past, Philip heard God tell him to chat to the man with the worried face (*chatter, chatter, chatter*). He ran as fast as he could to catch up with the chariot. The man was reading from God's special book, but he didn't seem to understand it very well.

'Do you understand what you're reading?' Philip called out.

'No, not really!' replied the man. 'I need some help. Perhaps you could come and sit with me in the chariot and explain what it all means.'

So Philip climbed into the beautiful chariot and chatted to the man *(chatter, chatter, chatter)*. He told the man how very much God loved him, and he told him all about Jesus. They chatted for ages *(chatter, chatter, chatter)*.

Slowly, the man's worried look was transformed into a big, beaming smile. 'Thank you so much for telling me all about Jesus! I'm going to ask him to be my special friend, too. And when I get home I'm going to tell everyone else the story that you've just told me. In fact, no one will be able to stop me talking about Jesus and about how much he has done for us!' *(Chatter, chatter, chatter.)*

Rhyme time

We can talk to God in a loud voice,
    to be heard by those around,
Or we can talk to God inside our head,
    without making a sound.
We can whisper to God, 'Thank you, Lord!'
    in a very, very small voice,
Or we can shout our prayers,
    'THANK YOU, LORD!'
    and make a joyful noise.

Song time

Sing the following words to the tune of 'Frère Jacques'. In the last line, the two words 'it's good' need to be sung on the same note.

I can say things.
I can say things.
So can you!
So can you!
Thank you, Lord, for voices.
Thank you, Lord, for voices.
It's good to talk!
It's good to talk!

'Two little eyes to look to God' JP 262. *(This could be used as a series song.)* 'He gave me eyes so I could see' verse 2, JP 74. *(This would also work as a series song.)*

Pray time

In the following prayer, the leader says each line in the appropriate manner and the children repeat the line in the same style. Don't be afraid to exaggerate the way you say the words: 'LOUDLY', 'softly', 'quickly' and 's l o w l y'.

We can talk LOUDLY!
We can talk softly.
We can talk *quickly!*
We can talk s l o w l y.
We can talk to our family.
We can talk to our friends.
Thank you, God, that we can talk.

Prayer collage
You will need:
magazine pictures of faces, round-ended scissors, PVA glue, backing-paper.

Help the children to cut out lots of pictures of mouths, or pictures of people talking, from old magazines. Alternatively, use the pictures cut out during the free-playtime at the beginning of your session. Stick them all onto backing-paper under the caption: 'Thank you, God, that we can talk.' Finish with an appropriate prayer, eg
Father God, we've made this collage because we want to tell you how much we enjoy talking. Thank you for giving us our voices. Amen.

Extra time

•*Mr Chatterbox*, by Roger Hargreaves (World International Publishing Ltd. ISBN 0-7498-0004-6)

•Arrange to phone someone using a mobile phone. Give an appropriate message: 'Have a nice day!' or 'Happy Birthday!' or 'Get well soon!' Hold up the phone and let the whole group call out their greetings.

•Make yoghurt pot telephones. Make a

hole in the base of two yoghurt pots. Tie them together with a length of string secured with a knot at either end. The children take it in turns to speak into their pot or to hold it to their ear to listen.

Adults too

Does your group meet in the morning? Why not invite the parents and carers to stay for a simple lunch one day? (Afternoon groups could start earlier and begin with lunch.) Sandwiches, crisps and yoghurts don't take long to organise. Invite someone to come in and give a five-minute talk to the group at the end of the meal. Parents with toddlers would be most interested in the Christian testimony of another young mum in a similar situation. Perhaps two of your Tiddlywinks leaders could take the children off to another room for a story or some singing, so that the parents can listen in peace.

Top tip

Put yourself in the place of a new family arriving at your group for the first time. How might they feel? It's not easy to walk into a toddler group and just start talking to someone. A registration table often works well. In this way, everyone gets spoken to immediately and can then be directed towards an activity, or introduced to someone with children of a similar age. Alternatively, have one leader who is free from other responsibilities and available to welcome people.

ACTIVITY PAGE: Photocopy page 19 for use

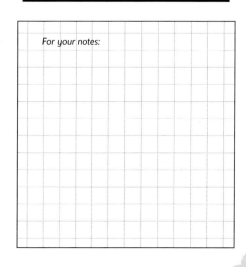

For your notes:

Thank you, God,
that I can see.

John 9:1–34

My
name

Make a mask!
1 Photocopy this page onto thin card.
2 Colour or decorate the mask shape.
3 Cut out.
4 Add a stiff piece of card on the
   back at one side as a handle.
5 Hold the mask in front of
   your eyes.

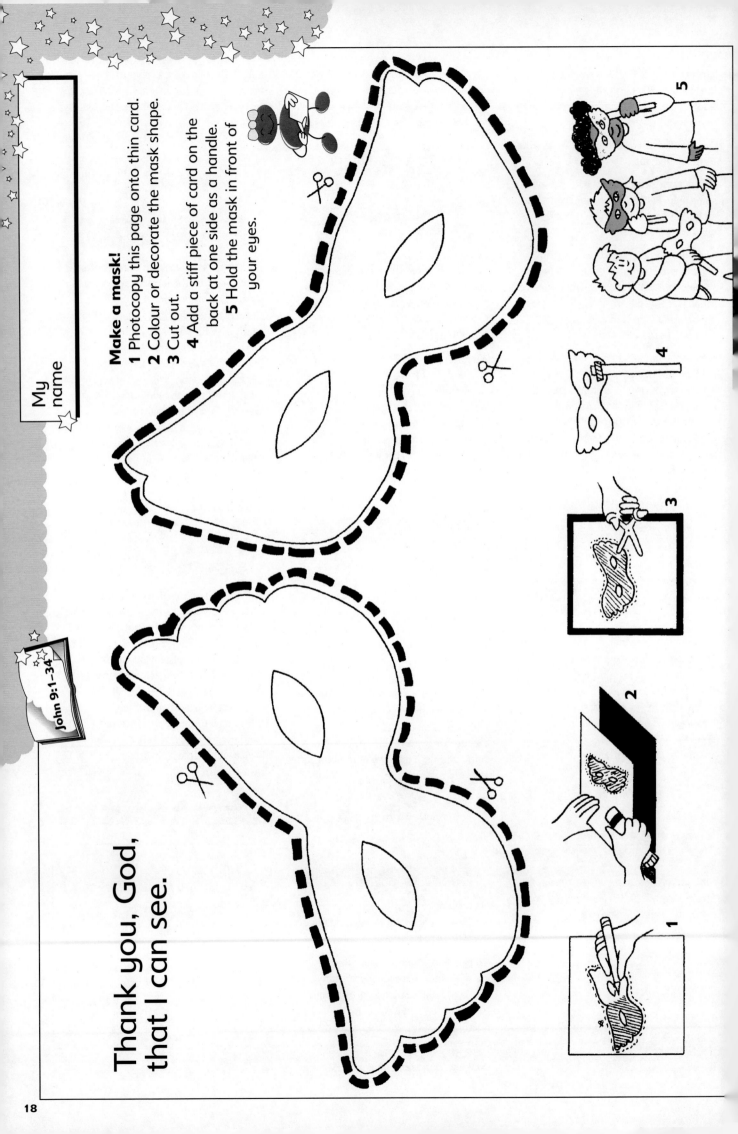

My name

Acts 8: 26-40

Thank you, God, that we can talk!

Can you colour in all the people who are talking?

19

I can hear

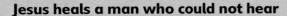

Mark 7: 31–37

Jesus heals a man who could not hear

Play time

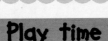

***You will need:** suitable music, plastic boxes, items to make a quiet or noisy sound, cuddly toys and dolls, strips of paper towel.*

Noisy table
Have a selection of free-play activities set out for when the children arrive. As this week is all about hearing and listening, why not have some music playing for the first few minutes? Invite children to visit 'a noisy table' at some point during this part of your session, and help them to create their own sound boxes. For this activity, you will need a number of empty plastic boxes and a selection of items to put inside. Let the children discover the different sounds they can create when they put wooden bricks, dried pasta, torn paper, coins, buttons, cotton wool and similar objets inside a box and shake it. Talk about which things make a loud noise, which ones a quiet noise, and which things make no noise at all.

Ear, ear!
In another corner, have a selection of cuddly animals and dolls for the children to play with. Talk about the different sizes and shapes of ears that they all have. Pretend that some of them have poorly ears, and let the children bandage them with strips of paper kitchen towel.

Look and chat
If you have a book corner, lay out one or two books about animals and talk about the different sounds that each animal makes. Include a shopping catalogue and talk about the sounds made by vacuum cleaners, food mixers, televisions etc.

no limit

Game time

***You will need:** carrier bags containing objects that make a noise, various objects*

for guess the noise, a toy that makes a continuous noise, or a mobile phone.

Noisy bags
Have ready a number of carrier bags with items in each one that make a

recognisable noise. One bag might contain *Duplo*, another knives and forks, a third two or three sheets of crumpled newspaper and a fourth a tambourine. Show the group the bags and shake each one in turn, for them to guess the contents by the noise. Talk about the kind of sound that the different objects make, eg *Duplo* rattles; knives and forks jangle; newspaper rustles, and tambourines jingle.

Hunt the noise
Hide a toy that makes a continuous noise, or a noisy alarm clock, so that the children search for it by listening. Alternatively, hide a mobile phone and, after the children have spent a minute searching, ring the number to help them find it!

3-5 mins

Making time

***You will need:** paper ear shapes, stapler, crayons, strips of thick paper, sticky tape.*

Headbands
Cut out plenty of ear shapes for the children to colour in – long, floppy dog

ears, big round elephant ears and tall, pointy rabbit ears work well. Staple the ears to a band of thick paper (about 5 cm wide), on which you have written the words: 'Thank you, God, for ears to hear.' Cover the reverse of the staples with sticky tape, to prevent the children getting scratched. Adjust the band to fit the child's head and fasten it with sticky tape.

10 mins

Story time

This week's story is punctuated with sound effects, to emphasise the wonder of having ears that hear. Make all the sound effects printed in italics and encourage the children and their carers to join in with each one. Explain that you are going to share a very special Bible story about a man who could not hear. The Bible doesn't give him a name, but you are going to call him Silas.

The sun was shining; the birds were singing *(tweet, tweet)* and the insects were buzzing *(bzzz, bzzz)*. It was a very hot day. Dogs were barking *(woof woof)*, donkeys were neighing *(ee-aww)* and people were rushing about in all directions *(footsteps)*. Everyone wanted to share the important news *('Jesus is coming! Jesus is coming!')*. Silas didn't know that Jesus was coming because his ears didn't work properly, and so he hadn't been able to hear the special news. Silas was quite deaf and because he couldn't hear he didn't speak very clearly either.

Some of his friends rushed up to him *(footsteps)* and grabbed him by the arms. 'Where are we going?' he asked. But he couldn't hear how his friends answered.

The group of friends took Silas to see Jesus. They were quite sure that Jesus

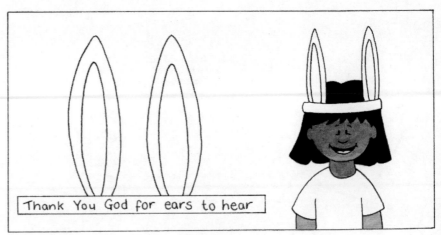

Thank You God for ears to hear

would be able to help him to hear well and speak clearly.

Jesus looked at Silas and smiled. The huge crowd of people who had come to see Jesus were very noisy *(chatter, chatter)*, so Jesus took Silas to a quiet place where only the birds could be heard *(tweet, tweet)* and the tiny insects *(bzzz, bzzz)*. Then, Jesus gently put his fingers into Silas' ears. Next, Jesus touched Silas' tongue. All at once, Silas could hear clearly. First, he heard Jesus' kind voice and then the birds *(tweet, tweet)* and the insects (bzzz, bzzz). He could even hear the crowd in the distance *(chatter, chatter)* and the sound of his neighbour's donkey *(ee-aww)*.

When Silas saw his friends again, they were amazed and delighted. 'Jesus is wonderful!' said Silas. 'Thank you for taking me to see him. Now I can hear well and speak clearly, too.'

Rhyme time

Say the following rhyme two or three times, inviting the children to repeat each noise or sound.

Fireworks go whiz and bang;
Saucepan lids clash and clang;
Car horns go beep, beep, beep,
And little birds twitter and cheep;
The man on the radio sings: 'La, la, la!'
A little lamb calls: 'Baa, baa, baa!'
The clock on the wall goes tic toc tic;
Nan's knitting needles go clickety click.
I can hear noises loud and clear
So I say: 'Thank you, God, for ears that
                                    hear!'

Song time

'Have you seen the pussy cat,' *KS 100*

'Two little eyes to look to God,' *KS 345.*
(This could be used as a series song.)

'He gave me eyes so I could see,' *JP 74.*
(This would also work as a series song.)

I hear thunder. I hear thunder.
Hark! Don't you? Hark! Don't you?
Pitter patter raindrops,
pitter patter raindrops,

I'm wet through; so are you!
(To the tune of *'Frère Jacques'*, Trad.)

Pray time

Ask all the children and their carers to tell you their favourite noise or sound and make a brief list. Weave all their suggestions into a response prayer, something like this...

We love the sound of tooting trumpets and banging drums, so we say...
Thank you, Lord, for ears that hear.

We love the sound of barking dogs and purring cats, so we say...
Thank you, Lord, for ears that hear.

 We love the sound of music on a CD, tape or radio, so we say... *Thank you, Lord, for ears that hear.*

We love happy sounds, like chattering, giggling and laughing, so we say...
Thank you, Lord, for ears that hear.

Extra time

• Look at a hearing aid and talk about how it can help people.

• Write your own version of Psalm 150, including all the instruments in your percussion box.

• Repeat a simple line of prayer over and over, starting very softly but getting louder every time, eg 'Thank you, God, that I can hear!'

• Make toy mobile phones out of small boxes; add stickers for the numbers and a pipe-cleaner for the antennae.

Adults too

What opportunities have the parents and carers in your group had to hear the good news? Why not invite the group to a forthcoming family or seeker service. Make sure that the

parents know exactly what to expect. They will want to know approximately how long the service will last (longer than 45 minutes can be very off-putting!), whether children are welcome and whether a crèche or Sunday group is provided. Many adults worry that they might be expected to say or sing something, or join in with spoken prayers. If possible, reassure them that they will be able to just sit back, listen and watch. Single parents who arrive with children can suddenly feel conspicuously alone when their children are whisked off to crèche or Sunday group. Offer to meet visitors outside and sit with them, if you feel this might help.

Top tip

Sometimes it can be a real battle to tell a story because toddlers are talking and the grown-ups are chatting to one another at the back of the group, which makes it very difficult for the children to hear. Don't be afraid to make it known that you expect everyone to listen to the story. You might like to start with: 'When all the boys are quiet and all the girls are quiet and all the grown-ups are quiet, then I'll begin...'

Alternatively, use a rhyme that begins loudly and ends softly. For example...
Point to the window; point to the door!
Point to the ceiling; point to the floor!
Clap your hands together: one, two, three.
Then, fold your arms and listen to me.

ACTIVITY PAGE: Photocopy page 24 for use

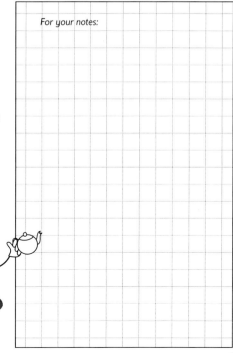
For your notes:

I can touch

Matthew 8:1–4

Jesus touches and heals a man with leprosy

Play time

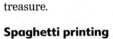

You will need: *aprons, newspaper, paint, paper, spaghetti, textured materials (eg cotton wool, silver foil, dried pasta) for the feely collage, glue, play dough.*

Set out two or three tables that the children can visit during the first part of your session. You will need an adult to supervise each table.

Finger painting
Cover a table with newspaper and provide aprons for the children. Give each child a splodge of paint in the centre of their paper and let them make spirals and patterns with their fingers. Talk about the wet, oozy feel of the paint.

Handprints
Help all the children to make a print of their two hands. Mount the picture on coloured card. Add their name and the date and give it to their families to treasure.

Spaghetti printing
Have a bowl of damp, cooked spaghetti. Add a squirt of paint and stir it up. Let the children dip their hands in and enjoy the feel of the cold, slimy pasta. Take out a handful and drop it onto paper. When you remove the spaghetti, you are left with a wonderful, squiggly print.

Feely collage
Draw a circle on a large sheet of backing-paper and then divide the circle into equal sections. Bring in a range of different things, all with a distinctive feel, for the children to stick onto the collage, eg shiny pieces of silver foil, soft cotton wool, bumpy corrugated cardboard, uncooked pasta spirals, grains of rice, scrunched-up tissue paper, rough sandpaper. Spread each section with PVA glue, one at a time, and let the children take turns to stick down the objects. Encourage them to think of suitable words to describe the feel of each object.

Play dough
Let the children explore their sense of touch by kneading, cutting and shaping play dough.

no limit

Game time

You will need: *a number of items inside boxes or bags, blindfold*

Guess the object
Put a number of different items into individual bags or plastic boxes. Ask the children to wear a blindfold and feel inside the bag or box to guess the identity of the mystery item. Choose items with a very distinctive feel, eg: soap, rice, water, cubes of jelly, cornflakes, moisturising cream, tissues, cotton wool.

Guess the person
Invite an adult to wear a blindfold and then guess who different group members are by gently feeling their hands, hair and faces. Once an adult has demonstrated the game, invite some of the children to come out and do the same.

8–10 mins

Making time

Story figures
You will need: *card gingerbread men shapes, crayons, wool, PVA glue.*

Cut out a simple gingerbread man shape for each child. Add a sad face, spots and blemishes to one side and give the other side a joyful smile and clean skin. Help the children to colour in their figures and glue on strands of wool for hair. Since these figures will be taken home, add a small caption to help those at home to understand something of what you are teaching in your *Tiddlywinks* group. For example: 'Jesus touched and healed the man with leprosy.'

10 mins

Story time

You will need: *the story figures made during 'Making time', or an old doll covered with blemishes, as described below.*

Invite the children to sit in a circle with their story figures on their laps, spotty side up. (If you haven't been able to make these story figures in your session, cover an old doll with spots and blemishes – draw red marks on sticky labels, or use a non-permanent red OHP pen to make the spots. At the appropriate moment in the story, remove the labels, or wipe off the marks with a damp cloth.)

Once upon a time, there was a man who had a nasty illness called leprosy. His skin was all ugly and sore. He couldn't use his fingers very well and he walked with a limp because the illness had damaged his foot. Nobody wanted to be friends with this man because they were all frightened of catching his illness. He had to live in a special village where other people with leprosy lived. He couldn't see his family and he couldn't go to work any more. Wasn't that a sad way to live? One day, the man heard that Jesus was coming to town.

'I must see Jesus!' he thought to himself. 'I know that Jesus can help me.'

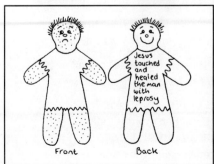

Front   Back

As he pushed his way through the crowd, everyone stepped back in horror. 'Stay away!' They all said. 'You're spreading germs. We don't want to catch leprosy.' The man managed to push his way right to the front and he knelt down at Jesus' feet.

'Jesus!' he said. 'I know that you have the power to make me well, if you want to.'

Jesus looked at him kindly. He put his hand on him and said, 'I do want to. Now you are well.' *(Turn over your story figure and ask the children to do the same. Or wipe off the marks on the doll.)*

At that moment, the man's leprosy disappeared. All his sore, ugly and uncomfortable skin vanished and he was left with new, clean, healthy skin. 'Thank you, thank you, thank you, Jesus!' he said. 'Everyone else was afraid to touch me, but you touched me and healed me.'

Rhyme time

Say this rhyme with the children two or three times, and mime feeling or touching each thing that is mentioned.

A new kitten feels warm and fluffy;
A birthday balloon feels light and puffy.
Mud pies feel thick and oozy;
My duvet feels warm and snoozy.
The kitchen table feels hard and shiny;
A hedgehog feels rough and spiny.
Birds' feathers feel soft and tickly;
A holly leaf feels sharp and prickly:
Play dough feels nice and squashy;
Bath water feels wishy washy.
There are many things I like to touch,
So I say: 'Thank you, God, very much!'

Song time

Sing the following words to the tune of 'Here we go round the Mulberry bush', encouraging the children to join in with appropriate actions.

This is the way we pat the dog,
    pat the dog, pat the dog.
This is the way we pat the dog,

when we use our fingers.

(Continue the song, adding new verses and actions. For example:)

This is the way we stroke a cat, splash the water, knead the bread.

Finish with the following verse:

This is the time to say: 'Thank you, God!
    Thank you, God! Thank you, God!'
This is the time to say: 'Thank you, God,
    'cos we can touch and feel.'

Also:

'Jesus' hands were kind hands' *KS 194*.

'Be careful, little hands, what you do' *JP 312*.
'Two little eyes to look to God' *KS 345 (This could be used as a series song.)*

'He gave me eyes so I could see' verse 3, JP 74. *(This would also work as a series song).*

Pray time

You will need: *paper, wax crayons, round-ended scissors, coloured backing-paper.*

Draw round each child's hand with a wax crayon and then, if time allows, cut out the shape. While you do this, ask the children to tell you about some of the things that they think feel nice. Encourage them to draw their suggestions onto their own hand shape, eg soft bubbles in the bath at night, squidgy play dough, fluffy toys, furry kittens, a soft, woolly jumper, a shiny pebble. Add captions to the children's pictures, where appropriate. Write the title: 'Thank you, God, that we can touch and feel!' onto a large sheet of backing-paper and stick all the hands in a pattern underneath. Finish by saying a prayer, thanking God for our sense of touch, and including all the children's ideas.

Extra time

•If you have an area suitable for wet play, or are able to meet outside, include sand and water in your range of activities designed to stimulate the group's sense of touch and feel.

•Make bread rolls from a packet mix and

 let all the children get involved in kneading the dough.

•Blow bubbles and challenge the children to pop them between their fingers.

•Use an ink stamp to make fingerprints and study the individual patterns.

Adults too

Explain to the parents and carers that as a Christian you believe in the power of prayer and often pray for people who are in hospital or unwell. Ask the adults if there is anyone special that they would like you to pray for now. Alternatively, suggest that folk come and chat to you over a cup of coffee if they would like you to mention a particular need in your personal prayers tonight, or in the church prayers on Sunday.

Top tip

When you gather together in a circle for story time, do you expect the children to sit on the hard floor? Why not bring in a special rug or blanket that you can unfold for use at story time. Children love special routines, so let the 'story rug' become part of your weekly routine.

ACTIVITY PAGE: Photocopy page 25 for use

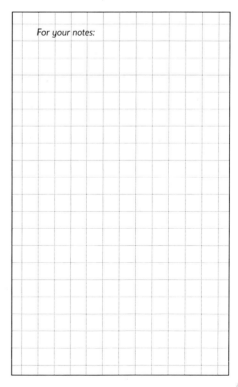

For your notes:

My name

Mark 7: 31–37

Thank you, God, for ears to hear all these noises loud and clear.

It's a noisy day in the park. Point to all the people making noises. What else is making a noise? Can you make that noise too?

Matthew
8:1–4

Thank
you, God,
that we
can touch
and feel!

Draw a circle
round all the
things that feel soft.
How do the other
things feel? Colour
in the pictures.

I can taste

Water into wine

John 2:1–10

God, that I can taste!' to the bird's tummy.

You will need: *toy teaset, squash, oranges, chopping board, sharp knife, squeezer, survey sheet and pen.*

Tea party

Have a selection of free-play activities set out for when the children first arrive. As this week is all about drinks and taste, you could include a toy teaset in one corner. Let the children have a little squash in the teapot, so that they can pour out pretend drinks for each other. A little adult supervision will be needed, to ensure that the children don't get wet!

Squeeze an orange

On another table, have two or three oranges and a hand squeezer, so that the children can make some real orange juice. Get an adult to cut the oranges in half on a chopping board, but before you do so, ask the children to guess how many pips will be inside. [TIP: Keep sharp knives out of reach.] Comment on the fact that every pip has the potential to grow into a tree. Let the children try their hand at squeezing the oranges and then encourage them to sample the juice. Invite all the children to visit this table at some point during the early part of your session.

Mini survey

While the children are enjoying free-play activities, go round with a young volunteer and ask all the adults and children to name their favourite drinks. Make a mini graph to show which drink is the most popular and reveal the results of your survey during circle time. During pray time (see below), thank God for all the drinks mentioned in the survey

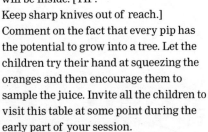

Game time

You will need: *plastic cups, three different*

drinks in cartons or jugs, wedding photos.

Mystery drinks

God has given us many different hot and cold drinks to enjoy. They all have their own unique taste or flavour, whether they are sweet, tangy, sour, juicy, bitter, refreshing, or just impossible to describe. Ask all the grown-ups to describe the taste of a cup of tea! Have ready a stack of plastic cups and three different drinks in numbered jugs. It is important that no one can see the colour of the drinks, so disguise the cartons or jugs. Invite adults and children to try a drink with their eyes closed; after they've tasted a drink, can they guess what it was? Can they tell the difference between two different drinks?

5 mins

Making time

You will need: *an enlarged copy of the bird shape below for each child, hole punch, crayons, bendy drinking straw.*

Thank You, God that I can taste!

Straw buddies

Photocopy the bird shape below onto thin card for each member of your group. Use a hole-punch to make the hole at the top and bottom. Encourage the children to colour the bird in bright colours. Write their names on the back and insert a bendy straw. Then, put the finished straw buddies aside for use during drink and biscuit time. Add the caption: 'Thank you,

Story time

You will need: *six small jugs that are not clear glass, a huge jug of water, blackcurrant squash, a glass tumbler.*

Pour a little juice into the six jugs beforehand. Set them out in a row (making sure that the children can't see that they have juice in). Tell the story as detailed below and at the appropriate moment pour water into the small jugs. Show the children how it has changed colour as you pour a drink into the glass.

Before you begin, tell the children that you will need their help because there is a lot of counting in the story. Use your fingers to count the numbers.

One day Jesus, his mother, Mary, and all his **1, 2, 3, 4, 5, 6, 7, 8, 9, 10, 11, 12** special friends were at a wedding party. It was a lovely party! There were **1, 2, 3, 4, 5** different sorts of bread to taste, **1, 2, 3, 4** different kinds of fruit and **1, 2, 3** different kinds of cake. Everyone was very happy – everyone, that is, except for the head servant, who was very worried. All the guests were shouting: 'We're really thirsty!' and he'd just discovered that all the wine had run out. What would everyone think? They might say it was the worst party they'd ever been to. The head servant went and asked Mary what he should do.

'I know!' she whispered. 'I'll ask my son, Jesus, because he always seems to be able to help people with their problems.' Mary went over to Jesus and his **1, 2, 3, 4, 5, 6, 7, 8, 9, 10, 11, 12** special friends. 'Please can you help these people?' she said. 'They've completely run out of wine.'

Jesus went into the kitchen and saw **1, 2, 3, 4, 5, 6** empty water jars.

'Fill all these jars with water,' he said, pointing to the **1, 2, 3, 4, 5, 6** jars. 'That's crazy!' thought the head servant. 'We've run out of wine, not water!' but the servants did as they were told. *(Pour water into the six jugs.)*

Soon, they heard an important guest shouting for another drink. Jesus told the servants to take the guest a drink from the water jar. *(Pour drink into glass.)* To their amazement, they saw that it was no longer water but deep, red wine. (Sample drink.)

'Delicious! This is the best wine I've ever tasted!' said the honoured guest. The head servant looked at Jesus and smiled. Jesus had certainly saved the day.

Rhyme time

Orange juice tastes rather nice,
Or fizzy cola with lots of ice.
A thick milkshake is really great;
A hot chocolate tastes first rate.
Grown-ups rather like a cup of tea,
Or a quick break with a hot coffee.
There are so many lovely things to drink.
God has been good to us, don't you think?

Jesus went to a party,
(Walk fingers up arm.)
He was having a lovely time,
(Roll hands over one another and clap.)
When someone came to him and said,
(Cup hand behind ear, as if listening.)
'We haven't any wine!'
(Shake head.)
Jesus told the servants,
(Mime giving instructions.)
'Fill lots of jars so tall.'
(Mime filling jars.)
But when they drew the water out
(Mime dipping a cup into jar
    and drinking.)
It was wine – the best of all!
(Rub tummy and smile.)

Song time

You will need: *music for songs*

Sing 'God is good to me,' and add an extra verse:

God is good to me; God is good to me.
He gives me jelly to fill my belly;
God is good to me.
God is good to us; God is good to us.
He gives us drinks,
which taste great, we think!
God is good to us.

Change 'Five currant buns in a baker's shop' to:

Five milkshakes in a coffee shop,
Thick and creamy, with a straw in the top,

Along came a boy *(or name of child)* with some money one day,
Bought a milkshake and took it away.
(Continue with 'Four milkshakes in a coffee shop…')

Pray time

(If appropriate, remind the children of all the drinks mentioned in the survey earlier, before praying:)

For fruity, juicy drinks –
Thank you, Lord!
For fizzy, refreshing drinks –
Thank you, Lord!
For warm, comforting drinks –
Thank you, Lord!
For yummy, scrummy drinks –
Thank you, Lord!
For all the wonderful flavours that tickle our taste buds –
THANK YOU, LORD!

Extra time

• Help the children to cut out pictures of food and drinks from magazines and supermarket leaflets. Stick all the pictures onto a sheet of backing-paper, under the title: 'Thank you, God, that I can taste all these lovely things!'

• Make simple wedding hats! A folded newspaper hat decorated with sticky shapes will be fine, or a paper plate hat with tissue paper flowers on top and ribbons cut from strips of crêpe paper. These could be made at the beginning of the session and worn during the story.

Adults too

Some of the foods that we enjoy are produced in conditions that we would consider unfair. Often the workers are exploited and barely earn enough to support their families. Why not contact a fairtrade organisation such as Traidcraft and consider running a stall of their fairly produced goods. Alternatively,

check out Café Direct, available at the main supermarkets. If you serve coffee at your weekly meeting you might like to consider switching to a fair trade brand.

Top tip

Make your drink and biscuit time a special part of your programme, rather than having refreshments available the whole time. You might like to have one set of toys out when the children first arrive, eg puzzles and bricks, dolls, teddies and books. Then enlist everyone's help to clear away these toys in time for circle time or story time. The children are more likely to listen to the story if there are fewer toys around to distract them. Follow the story with a drink and biscuit and then get out larger ride-on toys, or have music and movement, or percussion instruments and singing. This method also ensures that at the end of the session one or two people are not left with all the small toys to clear up.

Always make sure none of the children have food allergies eg nut allergies before you share food.

ACTIVITY PAGE: Photocopy page 30 for use

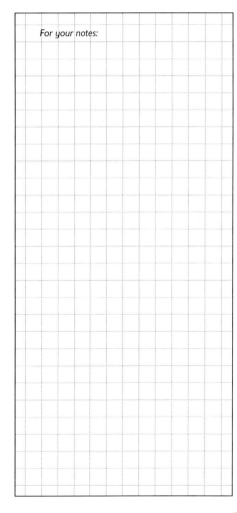

For your notes:

B6 All about me
I can move
Walking and leaping

Acts 3:1–11

Play time

You will need: *length of wallpaper, crayons or paint, marker pen.*

Footprints

At one end of your room, have a huge piece of wallpaper laid out, reverse side uppermost, on the floor. Invite the children to come up, one or two at a time, take off their shoes and socks, and stand in the middle of the paper while you draw round their feet. (If you have plenty of adult helpers, let the children dip their feet in paint and make a footprint. You will need a bowl of warm water and some old towels to wash and dry their feet afterwards.) Once they have made their prints, ask them what activities they enjoy that use their legs and feet. Write the title: 'Thank you, God, for…' at the top of the paper and then write their suggestions in large writing, graffiti-style, in the gaps on the paper, eg dancing, kicking a football, running and jumping, walking on tiptoe, gymnastics.

Music and movement
You will need: *music*

Play a lively pop song or a suitable nursery rhyme tape and encourage the children to copy your actions as you jump, bend, stretch and turn to the music. Play a simple game of 'Follow my leader', encouraging the children to skip, jog or march behind you, in time to the music.

Change the music for a praise tape and give out long lengths of crêpe paper for the children to twirl like streamers as they dance to the music.

Game time

You will need: *parachute / play canopy or king-size sheet.*

Parachute fun

Stand in a circle around a parachute or play canopy and ask all the children to hold on to the edge. Adults who are joining in will need to kneel down so that they are the same height as the children. Lift the sheet together and then lower it slowly. Once the children have got used to the rise and fall of the canopy, encourage them to run underneath and change sides, two or three at a time. Try calling out different categories, eg everyone wearing jeans, or everyone who ate cornflakes for breakfast, change sides. If you have a small group and no parachute, try the same activity using a large king-size sheet. When the game is finished, place the canopy on the ground and invite everyone to sit around the edge. Talk about the fun we can have running around and playing games. Thank God for giving us bodies that move in so many different ways.

Making time

You will need: *two chenille wires (pipe cleaners) per child.*

Help the children to twist the first chenille wire into the head and arms of a figure. Then pass the second chenille wire through the head; find the middle and bend it in half. Twist it two or three times to make the body, leaving the remaining ends as legs. Turn up the bottom half-centimetre to make the feet. (See illustration.)

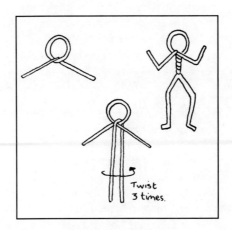
Twist 3 times.

Story time

You will need: *chenille wire figures made in 'Making time'.*

Invite all the children to sit down, with their chenille wire figures, to hear today's Bible story. Ask the children to bend their figures, so that they are also sitting down.

There was once a man with very poorly legs. The Bible doesn't tell us what his name is, but we shall call him Caleb. (Sit your own chenille wire figure on the palm of your hand.) Caleb couldn't walk, run, hop or skip like other people because his legs just wouldn't work. In fact, his legs had never worked, and so Caleb didn't know what it was like to be able to go wherever he wanted whenever he felt like it. He always had to wait for someone to carry him there. Each day, his friends carried him to the door of the Temple – a special church building where people went to talk and learn about and sing to God. Caleb held out his hands to beg for money from all the people going in. *(Raise the hands on your figure.)*

One day, two special friends of Jesus were on their way into the Temple. 'Please give me a coin,' said Caleb. 'I need money to buy food.'

Peter and John stopped and looked kindly at him. 'I don't have any money,' said Peter, 'but I will give you what I do have. In the name of Jesus, get up and start walking!'

Then Peter stretched out his hand and helped Caleb to stand up. *(Unbend your figure so that it is standing and suggest that the children do the same with theirs.)* At once, Caleb's feet and ankles became strong. He could jump, stand on one leg, bend down and touch his toes or stretch up high. *(Make your figure do some of these things and let the children copy.)*

Soon, Caleb followed Peter and John into the Temple. He started out walking, but then he was so happy that he couldn't stop running and jumping and praising God. All the people in the quiet Temple were amazed because they felt sure that he looked just like the beggar who couldn't move his legs. 'I am that man!' shouted Caleb, joyfully. 'I couldn't move my legs, but now look at me! God has healed me! Isn't God wonderful?'

Rhyme time

Encourage the children to shake, move and wobble their entire body as they say this rhyme with you:

Jelly on a plate, jelly on a plate,
Wibble, wobble, wibble, wobble,
Jelly on a plate!

March round the room to 'The Grand Old Duke of York', crouching low or marching on tiptoe, as appropriate.

Song time

Sing action songs:

'Head, shoulders, knees and toes'
'Hop, skip and jump'
'One finger, one thumb keep moving'
'I'm a dingle, dangle scarecrow'
'Hokey, cokey' *(traditional).*

Change 'Here we go round the mulberry bush' to the following words:

This is the way we touch our toes, touch our toes, touch our toes.
This is the way we touch our toes early in the morning.

Other verses might include: 'swing our arms', 'jump up and down', 'jog on the spot'.

Pray time

Help the children to rejoice in the movements of their body by fitting appropriate actions to this prayer. Encourage the children to join in loudly with the response: 'Thank you, Lord!'

For arms that swing and hands that clap,
Thank you, Lord.
For feet that stamp and toes that tap,
Thank you, Lord.
For legs that run and jump and walk,
Thank you, Lord.
For heads that nod and mouths that talk,
Thank you, Lord.
Because we can crouch down low, then jump up high,
Thank you, Lord.
Because we can stand on tiptoe and reach for the sky,

Thank you, Lord.
For giving us bodies that bend and stretch and move,
Thank you, Lord.

Extra time

 •Read *Topsy and Tim in the Gym* and hear how the twins enjoy learning new skills, or *Topsy and Tim Make a New Friend*, which takes a thoughtful look at disability. Both books are by Jean and Gareth Adamson (Ladybird Books. ISBN 0-7214-9767-5).

•If you can go outside, why not hold an impromptu mini sports event, with hopping, running, and crawling races, potato and spoon and running backwards races?

Adults too

Explain to the parents and carers that when you pray you often ask God for the things you need, for help in difficult situations, for healing for friends and family. The lame man in our story asked for money, but was given something far better. He was completely healed. Sometimes God does not answer our prayers in the way that we might expect because he knows what we really need, and what will be good for us, far more than we do.

Top tips

Sometimes toddler groups can be very hazardous places! Young babies lying on the floor can easily get run over by fast-moving infants on ride-ons. Badly driven doll's prams can mow down toddlers just taking their first steps! Put a line of chairs across the width of your room and, about a third of the way along, create a safe area where young babies can crawl and roll undisturbed. Insist that ride-ons are not allowed past the barrier of chairs.

If you are giving out the Jumping Jack activity page for children to make at home, you could give the mums or carers five paper fasteners each and ask the children to bring their finished figures back next week, to show the group.

ACTIVITY PAGE: Photocopy page 31 directly onto thin card for use

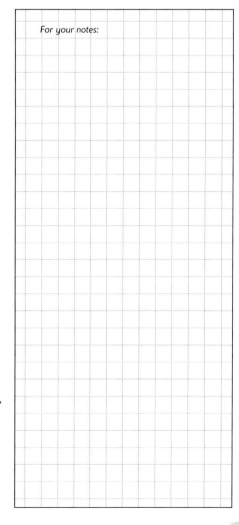

For your notes:

Thank you, God, that I can taste.

My
name

John 2:1–10

What do you like to drink best?
Draw it in the big cup.

Banana smoothies
Peel a small ripe banana.
Mash it up and let a grown-up put it in
a blender.
Add a spoonful of honey (or sugar, for
children under a year old).
Add a scoop of vanilla ice cream.
Add 250 ml of fresh cold milk.
Whiz it all up.
Pour into cups for two of you to share.
(You can use a hand whisk if you
haven't got a blender. It takes a bit
longer but it tastes just as good.)

Fizzy floats
Fill a cup about three-quarters full with
your favourite fizzy drink.
Add one scoop of vanilla ice cream.
Drink through a wide straw.

*Thank you, God that we can taste and
enjoy so many different things.*

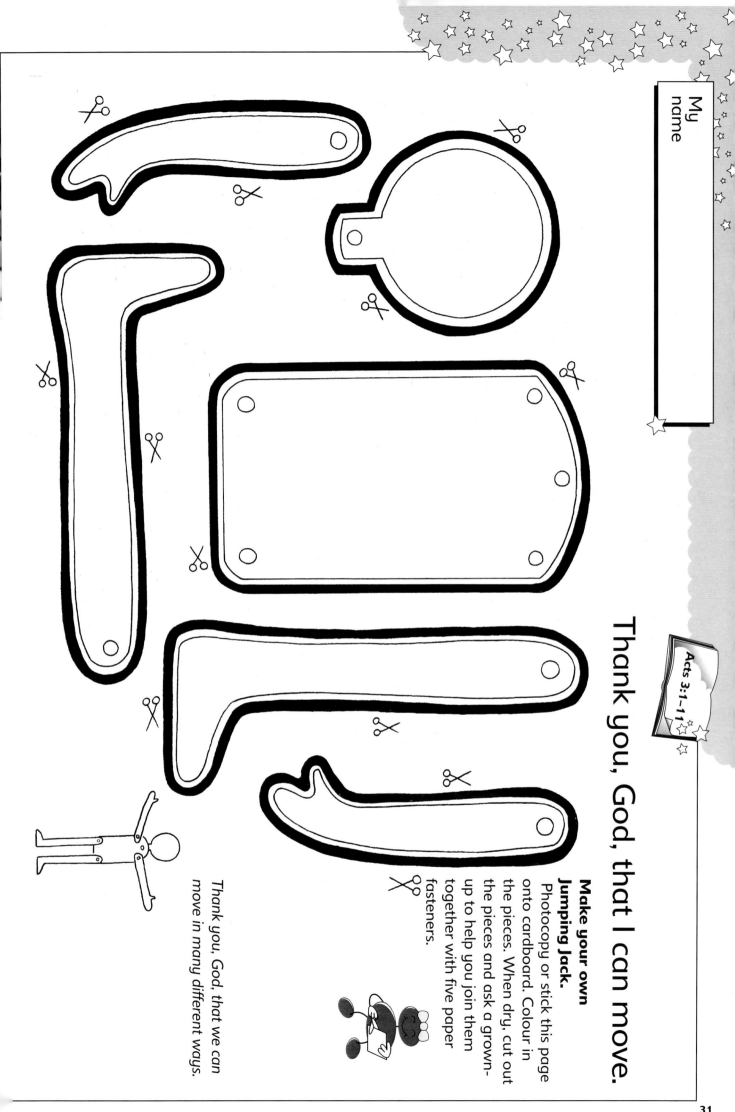

Acts 3:1–11

Thank you, God, that I can move.

Make your own Jumping Jack.

Photocopy or stick this page onto cardboard. Colour in the pieces. When dry, cut out the pieces and ask a grown-up to help you join them together with five paper fasteners.

Thank you, God, that we can move in many different ways.

B7 All about me
I can think
Solomon asks for wisdom

1 Kings 3:1–15;
2 Chronicles
1:1–12

Play time

You will need: music

Animal hop
Play some lively music and encourage the

children to hop, skip
and jump around the
room. Every time you
stop the music, they
must stand still and
listen while you
describe an animal –
then they must work out which animal it
is. Once everyone knows the animal,
encourage the group to move around like
that animal until you stop the music
again and give them a new description to
guess. For example:

I'm thinking of an animal with a fluffy
tail. It has long, furry ears. It likes to hop
and jump. *(Rabbit.)*

I'm thinking of an animal with a very
long nose. It has huge, flappy ears and an
enormous, grey body. *(Elephant.)*

I'm thinking of an animal that likes to
jump up and down. She keeps her baby in
a special pocket at the front. *(Kangaroo.)*

I'm thinking of an animal that some
people have at home. It needs lots of
walks. It has a waggy tail and a licky
tongue! *(Dog.)*

I'm thinking of an animal that likes to sit
on your lap. It purrs a lot and uses its
paws to wash its face. *(Cat)*

Puzzles
If you have a prolonged free-play session
at the beginning of your meeting, include
other activities – like puzzle trays,
jigsaws, matching and sorting games and
construction sets – that require the
children to think and work things out.

Game time

*You will need: prepared clues and
problems, as described below.*

Who am I thinking of?
Give the children three clues and then see
if they can guess whom you are thinking
of; it could be someone in the group, or a
famous character, eg
1. I'm thinking of someone who is
wearing a yellow T-shirt. She has blonde
hair. She has a baby brother. *(Child in
group.)*

2. I'm thinking of someone who lives in
Pontypandy. He drives a red engine called
Jupiter. He has a friend called Elvis.
(Fireman Sam.)

Problem solving
Explain to your group that we can use our
brains to think of ways to help people and
solve problems. Explain a problem to the
children and then discuss how it could be
solved.

1. Sally and Neeta have gone on the
playgroup picnic. When it comes to lunch-
time, Sally can't find her lunch-box
anywhere. What can be done?

*(Tell a grown-up. Help look for the lost
lunch-box. Sally and
the other children
could share their
lunches with her.)*

2. Tom was running
around and
accidentally knocked over the huge tower
of bricks that Bradley had built. Bradley
is very upset. What can be done?

*(Tom could say sorry and offer to help
build an even bigger tower. Tom could
invite Bradley to play a new game.)*

3. Kieran and Kate are both arguing over
a teddy bear. They both say: 'It belongs to
me!' What can be done?

*(Check for a name label. Tell a grown-up.
Put it away and check with their mums
later.)*

Making time

Remember pegs
You will need: wooden spring clothes
pegs, PVA glue, card, sticky shapes, clear
sticky-backed plastic.

Explain to your group that often grown-
ups have so much to think about that they
can be very forgetful! Ask the children
whether they have ever been shopping
with a grown-up who has said, 'I just can't
think what I need to buy!'

Cut some small pieces of card
(approximately 8 cm x 4 cm) and write the
word 'Remember' on each one.
Alternatively, print the word on a word
processor and let the youngsters stick it
onto their cards. Decorate the cards with
stars and sticky shapes and cover the
front with sticky-backed plastic. Stick
these cards onto a clothes peg with PVA
glue, to make a reminder peg that will
hold shopping lists, tickets, receipts and
so on. Clip a few pieces of paper into the
finished pegs and let the children take
them home as a present for their parents.

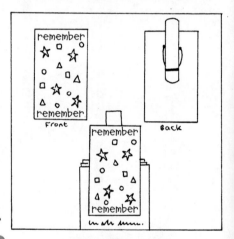

Story time

*You will need: dressing-gown and
cardboard crown, pillow.*

*Before you begin the story, put on a
dressing-gown and a crown to represent
King Solomon and tell the story in role.*

Hello, my name is King Solomon! One
night I was fast asleep in bed *(lie down
with head on pillow)* when I had a very
special dream. *(Sit up and explain.)* In my
dream I heard God saying to me,
'Solomon, you can ask for anything you
want and I will give it to you.'

Well, I was really surprised! At first, I just
didn't know what to ask for. Should I ask
God to make me amazingly rich, or
should I ask him to give me a long and

healthy life? I just didn't know what to say. Then, after I'd thought for a long, long time, I knew exactly what to ask for.

'Lord God!' I said. 'You have made me king, but I'm very young and I don't know very much about being a leader. There are so many people in my kingdom that I can't even count them all. Please make me wise and teach me the difference between right and wrong. Then I will know how to rule your people well.' I really wanted God to make me a wise king because that would mean that I'd be sensible and clever and able to think of good ideas to help people.

God was really pleased that I had asked for something that would help all the people in the kingdom, so he was very generous to me. He gave me the special wisdom that I'd asked for – and he also gave me silver and gold and a long life, too! I'm so glad that God gave me the ability to think of good ideas because I really enjoy being king, and people come from miles around to ask for my help and advice.

Rhyme time

God made my brain and he
   made my mind.
He helps me think of ways
   to be kind.
He gives me bright ideas every day
And he helps me think
   of kind words to say.
I'm glad that my brain can think for me;
God knew how important that would be.

Song time

You will need: *music for songs.*

Adapt 'Thank you, Lord, for this fine day,' JP 232 to:

Thank you, Lord, that I can think;
Thank you, Lord, that I can think;
Thank you, Lord, that I can think
   of many good ideas.
Alleluia, praise the Lord!
Alleluia, praise the Lord!
Alleluia, praise the Lord!
Right where we are.

Sing the following words to the tune of 'Peter hammers with one hammer, one hammer, one hammer...' (traditional):

Solomon thought of good ideas,
   good ideas, good ideas,
Solomon thought of good ideas,
   all day long.
We can think of bright ideas,
   bright ideas, bright ideas,
We can think of bright ideas, all day long.
Thank you, God, for brains to think,
   brains to think, brains to think,
Thank you, God, for brains to think,
   all day long.

Pray time

Explain to the group that you are going to say a prayer and you want them to repeat each line after you. In this prayer, we are going to thank God for our brains that can think. Ask the children where they think their brains might be. Suggest that as they say this prayer they close their eyes to help them concentrate and place their hands on either side of their head.

Thank you, God, for giving us brains that can think.
Help us to think of ways to help other people.
Help us to think of bright ideas.
Help us to think kind thoughts.
Amen.

Extra time

•Play 'Hot and Cold', which requires basic listening and thinking skills. Send a child out of the room with an adult and hide an agreed object for them to find. When they return, the whole group says: 'Warm... getting warmer... very warm... hot... boiling hot...' as they come close to the object, and: 'Getting cooler... cold... very cold...' as they move away. Once the object is found, send another adult and child outside the room.

Adults too

Sometimes, bringing up young children can feel a little like being thrown in at the deep end. Solomon prayed for wisdom in leading his people; we need to pray for wisdom in bringing up our children. Many young parents live far away from their own families and need on-the-spot support when they face some of the difficulties involved with raising a family: 'Why does my child bite other children?' or 'Should I let my baby have an MMR jab?' or 'Why hasn't my little one shown any interest in using his potty?' Be prepared to offer a listening ear and a shoulder to cry on. Why not have a mini-library of parenting books to borrow such as: *The Parentalk Guide to the Toddler Years,* Steve Chalke, Hodder and Stoughton. *Faith in the family*, David Durston, The Bible Society

Top tip

Show the children that you think about them on their special days. Make sure that you have a register with the children's birthdays marked in it and a stock of cards ready to give out. Why not establish a birthday routine? Perhaps you could have a pretend cake with candles to blow out. One 'Mums and Tots' group from Whittlesey Baptist Church in Cambridgeshire always sings happy birthday and then adds this extra verse:

Birthday greetings today,
May God bless you, we pray!
Live for Jesus, dear... *(name of child)*
May he guide you always.

ACTIVITY PAGE: Photocopy page 36 for use

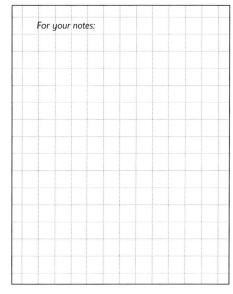

For your notes:

B8 All about me
I can make

Jeremiah and the potter

Jeremiah
18:1-4

Play time

Salt dough

You will need; 300 g (10 oz) plain flour, 300g (10 oz) salt, 1 tbsp vegetable oil, 200 ml (7 fl oz) water, a bowl, paper-clips, pastry cutters, rolling-pins, an oven (optional), paper plates (optional).

Make up a batch of salt dough in advance. If covered, the dough can be kept in the fridge for a week or two, which makes advance preparation easy. To make the dough, mix together all the ingredients listed above in a bowl. [TIP: Add a touch more oil if the mixture does not seem suitably stretchy; add extra flour if it is too wet.] Sprinkle a little flour onto your worktop and place the dough on top. Knead the dough until it becomes supple and stretchy. The dough is now ready to be moulded into different creations, or cut into shapes with pastry cutters. Shapes can be stuck together with water, eg to stick a head to a body.

Give each child their own lump of dough and let them mould it in any way they choose. After a while, introduce rolling-pins, cutters and other small tools. Use a gingerbread man cutter to make salt-dough people and use the point of a pencil to mark eyes, nose and mouth. Alternatively, help children to make the initial letter of their name. Sink a paper-clip into the top, which will set firm during cooking, to make a simple hook, so that once the initial is painted it can be hung on the wall. If you intend to cook the dough shapes during your session, you will need to preheat your oven to 180º C/350 ºF/Gas mark 4. Put all the dough shapes onto a baking tray (well separated as they will spread) and bake in the oven for about twenty minutes, or until they are hard. Thick, dense shapes will take a while longer. If you run out of time during your session, or do not have an oven, put the shapes on paper plates and let the children take them away to finish off in their oven at home. Alternatively, ask a leader to cook the shapes; then, next week let the children paint them and take them home.

Game time

You will need: several home-made articles, a magazine picture cut up into several pieces.

Guess who made it?

Ask one or two leaders to bring in things that they or a member of their family have made, eg a *Lego* model, a painting, a hand-knitted jumper, a clay model or some home-made biscuits to share later. Ask the children if they can guess who made each thing and how it was made.

Make a picture

Cut up a large magazine picture into ten or twelve pieces and hide the pieces around your room. Ask the children to find the pieces and bring them to the front, where they can all help to make up the picture. Comment on the fact that it's fun to make things together.

Making time

You will need: old brown envelopes, coloured paper, thin card, grey modelling clay, terracotta pots, poster paint or emulsion, sponges, varnish.

Make flowerpot greetings cards

Cut flowerpot shapes out of old brown envelopes, a stalk and leaf from green paper, and flowers from brightly coloured paper. Let the children stick the pieces together to make a card for a special friend. The finished card looks particularly effective if the flower is slightly larger than the backing card.

Make clay pencil pots

Use grey modelling clay to mould cubes, spheres or letter shapes. Once the children are happy with their shape, help them to poke a pencil into the top in five or six places, to make pencil-shaped holes. Leave the pen/pencil holder to dry until next week and then paint and varnish it. [TIP: This makes a super Father's Day present!]

Story time

You will need: a large, 'squashable' pot made out of Plasticine, play dough or salt dough, apron.

In advance, make a large pot out of Plasticine, play dough or salt dough, and place it on a round tray. Put on an apron and tell the story of Jeremiah visiting the potter's shop from the potter's point of view. Since this is a difficult passage to tackle with pre-school children, the following narrative only draws on the first four verses of chapter 18.

I really like making pots. Here's one that I made earlier… Of course, it's not finished yet – it has to be baked in a hot oven, so that it will go hard – but I really like the shape of this one; it's turned out rather well!

God's special messenger, Jeremiah, came to visit me in my workshop last week. He was very interested in all my pots, and he inspected them very closely. Would you like a closer look at this pot?' *(Pass the pot around on its tray and let the children look at it. Prearrange with one of the leaders or adults that when the pot comes to them, they will lift it off the tray for a closer look and then fumble and drop it. This leader should apologise profusely for dropping the pot and wonder aloud whether to throw the mangled remains in the bin. Ask the children what they think you should do. No doubt someone will suggest that you should remake it – congratulate this child and continue the story.)*

You're quite right! With a little time and effort I can reshape this pot until it's just as good as new, and then no one will know that it went all wrong and out of shape.

Do you know what? Jeremiah was especially interested in the pots that I was making that went all wrong. He really liked watching me squash up the clay into a round ball and start all over again.

Jeremiah says that people are a bit like pots and God is like a potter. Just like I decide what I want my pots to look like when I pick up my piece of clay and start to work on it, God knows the kind of people he wants us to be. And just like I mould and make my clay into the right shape, God works in our lives helping us to grow and change too so that we can be beautiful and useful, just like one of my pots.

Now I'm going to make a fresh start with this pot; I'm sure that I can reshape it and make it look really beautiful again.

Rhyme time

If possible, say the rhyme below while the children mould shapes out of play dough or Plasticine.

Pat-a-cake, pat-a-cake, baker's man,
Bake me a cake as fast as you can.
Pat it and prick it and mark it with B,
And put it in the oven for baby and me.

It's great to create!
God made animals (*mime an elephant*),
Fish and birds too (*mime fish and bird shapes with hands*),
Many different kinds,
Enough to fill a zoo (*stretch out arms wide*).
God made the earth
(*make a round circle*),
The sky (*point up*)
and the sea (*wavy hands*),
God made people (*point to others*)
And God made me (*point to self*).
God made us to enjoy making things too (*mime building with hands*);
It's great to create and make something new (*thumbs up*).

Song time

'Who put the colours in the rainbow?' *KS 386*
'God loves you just the way you are' *GBT 33*

'God made the world' *GBT 37*

Sing the following words to the tune of 'The wheels on the bus…'

God made me so I can walk and run,
    walk and run, walk and run,
God made me so I can walk and run,
    all day long (*running on the spot*).

Other verses: God made me so I can build and make (*one fist on top of the other, building*); God made me so I can love and care (*cross hands on heart then open arms wide*).

Pray time

You will need: coloured paper triangles; ribbon or a strip of crêpe paper, crayons, stapler.

Give everyone a paper triangle and ask the children to draw a picture on it of something they like making, eg a picture of themselves making biscuits, making a *Plasticine* model, or making a collage. Add captions to their pictures, eg 'Sam making a model', 'Charlotte making cakes'. Fold over the top 3–4 cm of the triangles and then staple them to a strip of crêpe paper or ribbon, to look like festive bunting. Offer the prayer bunting to God in a final prayer that incorporates some of the children's ideas, eg

Father God, thank you for making our beautiful world and thank you for making us. We're so glad that you made us to enjoy making things, too. Thank you that we can have fun making cakes and biscuits, pictures and collages, models and greetings cards…

Extra time

• Make decorated biscuits by covering plain biscuits with icing and chocolate drops.

• Use pastry cutters to make star- and circle-shaped jam sandwiches to enjoy at drink and biscuit time.

Adults too

Today's story carries a powerful message for the adults, too. If you run a pram service that includes an adult spot, you might like to make these points: Jeremiah's visit to the potter's house reminds us that we are like clay pots that are still being moulded. When we make mistakes and go wrong, God wants us to turn to him and to tell him that we are sorry; then he will forgive us and lovingly remould us, just as a potter remoulds a clay pot that goes wrong. Making a pot on a real potter's wheel is no easy task. If the clay is not centred in the middle of the wheel, the pot turns out to be very lopsided and wobbly. If there is a hard lump in the clay, that will also make it difficult to mould the pot successfully. God wants to mould our lives into something beautiful, and for this to be possible we need to centre our lives on Jesus. If we are carrying with us past problems and grievances, we need to ask God to help us deal with these first, so that we can move on and make a fresh start.

Top tip

Make and bake a salt dough figure in advance, so that you can time how long the whole process takes and have an example to show the children. Cover the table with a PVC cloth or a sheet of polythene to restrict the mess. Alternatively, work outside! Give the children old shirts, with the collars and cuffs cut off, to wear back-to-front as aprons for messy play.
For further craft ideas, useful tips and recipes for making play dough and home-made baking clay, check out: *Here's one I made earlier…* compiled by Kathryn Copsey (ISBN 0-86201-981-8) and *Here's another one I made earlier…* compiled by Christine Orme (ISBN 9 781859 993385), both published by Scripture Union.

ACTIVITY PAGE: Photocopy page 37 for use

For your notes:

My name

1 Kings 3:1–15;
2 Chronicles 1:1–12

I can think.

Carlton and Kirsty have been thinking of ways to help other people.

What have they been doing? Think about what you could do to help. Draw yourself here.

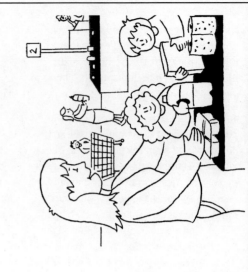

Father God, please help me to think of ways to help other people.

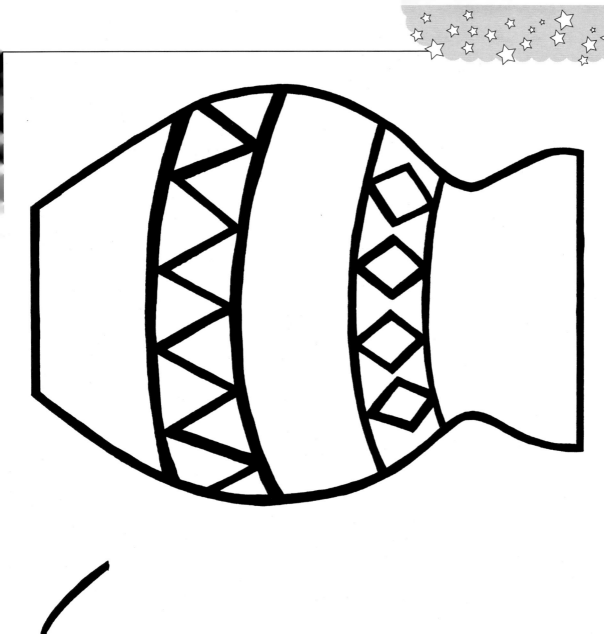

Thank you, God, for the fun of making things.

Jeremiah 18:1-4

The potter has made you a pot. Colour it in, as brightly as you can. Then draw your own pot by the side. What shape will it be?

37

B9 All about me
I can smell
Jesus is anointed

John 12:1–8

Play time

You will need: *free-play toys, wet wipes, talcum powder, towel, baby doll, plastic bath, warm water, bubble bath, face pictures, variety of paper nose shapes, glue sticks, crayons.*

Fragrant feet!
Encourage the children to go barefoot for this first part of the session, while they choose which toys they would like to play with. When you stop and clear away the toys for story time, bring out a big tub of wet wipes to 'wash' the children's feet. Then dry their feet with a towel, sprinkle them with talcum powder and offer them a dab of perfume before helping the children to put their shoes and socks back on. Comment on the fact that it feels great to have clean and fragrant feet!

Choose a nose
Draw some very simple faces without noses for the children to colour in. Have a variety of noses available on separate pieces of paper for the children to select and stick down.

Bathing baby
If you have an area suitable for wet play, or are able to meet outside, fill a baby bath with warm water and let small groups of children bathe toys and dolls. Add a little bubble bath to make fragrant bubbles.

Game time

You will need: *five things to smell, all hidden in plastic tubs or paper bags; clown face with detachable nose, and Blu-tack.*

Guess the smell
Prepare a selection of items for the children to smell, eg an orange, toothpaste, soap, crisps, chocolate, an apple. Hide the items in separate bags and ask the children to close their eyes before they sniff the item. If they know the answer, let them whisper it into your ear so that the other children can work it out

for themselves when it's their turn.

Talk about how very useful our noses are: they can tell us when something is good enough to eat, or if it is rather old and past its best. They can also smell burning and warn us of a fire. When we taste food, we rely on our sense of smell. If we have a cold and a blocked nose, our food doesn't taste nearly so good.

The clown's nose
Draw a simple picture of a clown with a large, red, detachable nose and a piece of *Blu-tack* on the back. Blindfold the children or ask them to close their eyes tightly and turn them round once. Then ask them to fix the nose back on the clown, in the style of 'Pin the tail on the donkey'.

10 mins

Making time

You will need: *pictures showing the outline of a perfume bottle, with the caption: 'Thank you, God, that I can smell so many lovely things!' Also, gold or silver paper bottle top shapes, pot-pourri, PVA glue.*

Give the children a simple outline of a perfume bottle and help them to glue some scented pot-pourri inside the shape. As a finishing touch, add a gold or silver paper bottle top.

10 mins

Story time

You will need: *perfume; dressing-gown or biblical tunic.*

Ask a leader to go barefoot, wear a biblical-style costume and play the part of Jesus, while you play the part of narrator-cum-disciple, and walk, talk and mime your way through the story. Encourage the leader playing Jesus to interact with you and chip in with thoughts and feelings.

Jesus has walked a long way and he's feeling hot, tired and dusty. *(Walk three or four times round the room, following Jesus with the children, as you tell this first part of the story.)* He is looking forward to reaching the home of Mary, Martha and Lazarus. They are very special friends, and he is particularly anxious to see Lazarus again – when Lazarus was really poorly, Jesus brought him back to life.

Are we nearly there yet, Jesus? It is a very, very long way. I'm really looking forward to my meal; Martha is an excellent cook. Oh look, here's their front door now! *(Knock on the door.)*

It's OK, everyone: they're ready for us; we just have to wash our hands and faces in the water tub outside. *(Everyone mimes washing face and hands.)* I think I'll splash a little water over my feet, too; they're feeling really tired and dusty – that's the trouble with open sandals!

How are you feeling, Jesus? Do your feet hurt? OK, we can all go in now. Let's sit in a circle; then Martha will know that we're ready to eat. *(All sit down.)* Wow! I'm tired! Do your feet still feel tired and sore, Jesus?

Oh look, here comes Mary. She's got a bottle of perfume with her – I wonder why. *(Produce a bottle of perfume and invite a child to play the part of Mary.)* Look! Mary's kneeling down in front of Jesus and she's pouring the expensive perfume on Jesus' feet! *(Invite the child to do this.)* How does that feel, Jesus? I suppose that Mary wanted to do something very special for Jesus, something that would show him how much she loved him and cared about him.

Oh look! Mary is drying Jesus' feet with her hair. She must love Jesus very much! I guess the perfume has made Jesus' tired feet feel good again. The whole room is filled with the smell of Mary's perfume now. Later on today, whenever I smell that perfume in the air, I'll remember just how much Mary loves Jesus.

Rhyme time

Let everyone try smelling some scented soap, or fragrant perfume. Then say the following rhyme two or three times with the children, pointing to a different person each time:

Roses are red, violets are blue,
Flowers smell lovely – and so do you!

Safety note: remember that some children may have skin allergies to scented products.

Thank you God
Thank you, God, that I can smell
So many things so very well.

The wake-up smell of hot, fresh toast,
The inviting smell of Sunday roast.

Thank you, God, that I can smell
So many things so very well.

Sausages and bacon smell so nice,
Or warm cookies with sugar and spice.

Thank you, God, that I can smell
So many things so very well.

The Elephant
An elephant goes like this and that
(use an arm to make an elephant trunk),
He's terribly big and terribly fat
(indicate size with hands and arms).
He's got no fingers and he's got no toes
(waggle fingers, hold up foot),
But goodness, gracious what a nose
(show elephant trunk again)!

Song time

'Put your finger on your head (on your nose),' (*Okki Tokki Unga* 27, A & C Black, London. ISBN 07136 4078 2) Change the words of 'The wheels on the bus go round and round' to:

The fruit in the bowl smells really good, really good, really good.
The fruit in the bowl smells really good.
Thank you, God!

Make up other verses to include some of the smells that the children like best, eg:

The bacon in the pan smells rather nice…
The biscuits in the tin smell really great…
The flowers in the garden smell beau-ti-ful…

Pray time

You will need: *pen and paper.*

Ask your group to tell you about some of their own favourite smells. List or draw their ideas and weave them into a simple response prayer, similar to the one below. Encourage the children and adults to join you in saying: 'Thank you, Lord!' whenever they hear the words 'We want to say...'

For the smell of freshly baked bread and cakes,
We want to say... Thank you, Lord!

For fruity smells, like oranges and lemons,
We want to say... Thank you, Lord!

For perfume and bubble bath,
We want to say... Thank you, Lord!

Extra time

•Make paper plate masks with silly noses. Cut holes for the eyes and mouth and then use kitchen roll tubes, fromage frais pots, empty matchboxes, segments of egg cartons or similar to create different-shaped noses. Make a small hole on either side and attach shirring elastic to keep them on.

•Use face paints to decorate the children's noses. You could try red clown noses or pink kitten noses, complete with whiskers across the cheeks.

•Bring in lots of different cuddly toys, zoo animals or similar and talk about the different kinds of noses animals have. Many animals have a better sense of smell than we do. A dog can follow someone just by the smell they leave behind.

Adults too

Mary showed Jesus just how much she loved him through her generous and thoughtful act. She didn't care what other people might think or say; she simply focused her attention on Jesus. Sometimes it's difficult to tell others about Jesus; we feel tongue-tied or embarrassed, but if we focus on Jesus, he will give us the right words and the right opportunities. Pray that God will give you the chance to share your Christian faith with the parents and carers who come to your group. Judas criticised Mary for wasting the perfume, but Jesus stood up for her. He will also be there to strengthen us when we face criticism for our beliefs.

Top tip

While we are on the subject of noses and smells, what kind of facilities do you provide for changing nappies? Invest in a changing mat and have a basket with wet wipes, tissues, disinfectant spray and nappy sacks on hand. Most carers carry these things with them, but it's wise to be prepared for those who run out or forget. All too often, meeting-places make no provision for infant visitors, which is unwelcoming for both carer and baby. For older children, try to provide a toilet seat and potty, and a sturdy stool to help them reach the sink.

ACTIVITY PAGE: Photocopy page 42 for use

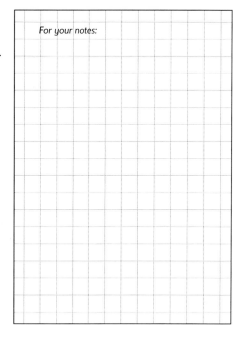

For your notes:

I can grow

Samuel

1 Samuel 3

Play time

Dressing up

You will need: dressing-up clothes of all sizes, height chart and marker pen.

Have ready a selection of free-play activities, including a big box of dressing-up clothes to suit all sizes and ages. Include some baby clothes that will be much too small for the children but which might fit a baby doll, and some huge grown-up clothes that will be too big. Try to include a big pair of wellington boots and let the children have a go at walking across the room in them. Make up situations for them to dress up for, eg 'It's a cold day! Let's all get dressed up and go to the park!' Or: 'Let's get dressed up for a special party!'

Just for fun, play some suitable music and let the children parade in their dressing-up clothes. Invite an adult to provide a commentary, describing the clothes that are worn!

Talk about the fact that some of the baby clothes are much too small, and the children have grown out of them; other clothes are far too big, and it will be some years before they grow into them. Point out that children grow, just a little, every single day – even when they are asleep in bed.

Height chart

Fix a length of wallpaper to the wall, reverse side uppermost, and label it at 5 cm intervals from the floor upwards. Invite the children to come up, one at a time, and stand against your height chart, while you mark their height and write their name at the appropriate level.

Game time

You will need: three pairs of shoes for a baby, child and adult.

Before you sit down in a circle, borrow a pair of shoes from a baby, a child and an adult and hide the six shoes around your room. Explain to the children that these three folk have lost their shoes and ask for some help to find them. Once all the shoes have been restored to their owners, ask the children how they managed to match the shoes to the right people. Once upon a time, the adult would have been able to wear the child's shoes, and the child would have been able to wear the baby booties, but now their feet have grown much bigger. Ask the children if they have had any new shoes recently, and make a point of admiring them. Did they grow out of the old shoes? Move on to talk about growing out of other clothes. Bring out a tape measure and compare the length of legs and arms in children of different ages.

Making time

You will need: cress seeds; kitchen towel or cotton wool, scissors, plastic plates or egg shells, felt pens, water.

Cress people

Cut sheets of white kitchen towel into simple people shapes. A gingerbread man shape approximately four sheets thick works well. Put the paper shapes onto plastic plates and let the children dampen them with water. Help them to sprinkle cress seeds evenly over the whole shape. Let the children take the plates home to watch the seeds grow. Remind them to keep the paper towel damp. After three or four days, they will be able to see their cress person begin to sprout and grow. Point out that in our own way we are growing too.

Cress heads

Use half an eggshell stuffed with damp cotton wool as another fun way to grow cress. Help the children to draw a face on the eggshell in felt-tip pen and sprinkle the cress seeds over the damp cotton wool. As the cress sprouts, the 'egg head' grows hair!

Story time

As you tell the following story, encourage the children to join in with the call: 'Samuel, Samuel!' and the reply: 'Here I am! What do you want me to do?'

Eli, the priest, was very old and stiff. He couldn't see very well, and he found it difficult to bend down when he dropped something. Eli was very pleased that he had young Samuel with him to help him look after God's Temple.

Whenever Eli needed Samuel, he would call: **'Samuel! Samuel!'** and Samuel would come running. **'Here I am, Eli!'** Samuel would say. **'What do you want me to do?'** When Samuel was young, Eli would ask him to sweep the floor in God's special Temple; when he grew a little older, he would ask him to polish the beautiful silver decorations, and when he grew a little older still, Eli would send him to town, to take important messages. Samuel enjoyed growing up in God's Temple.

One night, Samuel was asleep in bed when he heard someone calling: **'Samuel, Samuel!'**

Who do you think it was?

Samuel went straight to Eli's room. **'Here I am,'** he said. **'What do you want me to do?'** Eli woke up with a start. 'No, no! I didn't call you. Go back to bed!' So that's just what Samuel did.

Soon, he heard the voice again: **'Samuel, Samuel!'**

Samuel got out of bed and went back to

Eli's room. **'Here I am,'** he said. **'What do you want me to do?'**

'Uh! What?' grunted Eli. 'No, I didn't call you; go back to sleep.' So that's just what Samuel did.

Soon, he heard the voice calling him again. **'Samuel, Samuel!'**

He got out of bed and went back to Eli's room for a third time. **'Here I am,'** he said. **'What do you want me to do?'**

This time, Eli realised that it must be God who was calling Samuel, so he said, 'Go back to bed and if you hear the voice again, say: 'I'm listening, Lord. **What do you want me to do?'**

So that's just what Samuel did. When he heard the voice calling him a fourth time: **'Samuel, Samuel!'** he replied: 'I'm listening, Lord. **What do you want me to do?'** And this time God spoke to Samuel and gave him a very important message.

The next morning, Samuel got out of bed and he remembered everything that had happened. God had given him an important message in the middle of the night. Samuel felt very grown-up indeed.

Rhyme time

Begin by reading this rhyme to your group. Then read it a second time, with the children helping you to make up an appropriate action for each line. Finally, say the poem with actions, and see if the children can fill in the last word of each line from memory.

First I was a baby and really rather small.
Then I grew a little bit and
    started to crawl.
Soon I was a toddler; if I wobbled
    I would fall.
I could only take a couple of steps,
    not many at all.
Now I've grown older, I can run, jump and
    kick a ball
And when I stand up straight – you'll see
    I've grown quite tall!

Song time

You will need: music for songs.

Sing the following words to the tune of 'Jesus loves me, this I know, for the Bible tells me so'.

God has made me, this I know
And he loves me 'n' helps me grow.
We are growing every day
And God helps in every way.
Yes! God has made us! Yes! God has made us! Yes! God has made us!
And he helps us to grow.

'Have you seen the pussy cat, sitting on the wall?' *KS 100 (especially chorus)*
'If I were a butterfly' *KS 128*
'Whether you're one' *KS 384*
'Stretch and grow, reach for the stars' From *Hop, Skip and Jump (ELC)*

Pray time

Invite the children to join in with the following prayer by crouching down on the ground when they hear the words 'Father God…' and then slowly unfolding and growing upwards as they say the words 'Help us to grow closer to you.'

Like a tree that grows tall and stately,

Father God… Help us to grow closer to you.

Like a field of crops growing thick and golden,

Father God… Help us to grow closer to you.

Like a flower growing towards the sun,

Father God… Help us to grow closer to you.

Like fruit growing ripe and rosy,

Father God… Help us to grow closer to you.

Extra time

Show the children some photos of yourself as a baby, a toddler, a young child, a teenager and so on. Talk about the fact that each year you grew just a little older and a little taller.

Bring out a collection of dolls or teddies and ask the children to put them in size order. Work out which is the tallest and

most grown-up doll, and which is the smallest and youngest.

'Barney, what will I be when I grow up?' published by Egmont Children's Books Ltd. (ISBN 0–434–80711–7)

Adults too

Books for adults
Check out Scripture Union's and CPAS' 'Growing in faith' series. The series comprises four books for all those involved in children's and family evangelism:
Children Finding Faith, by Francis Bridger, ISBN 1 85999 323 0
Bringing Children to Faith, by Penny Frank, ISBN 1 85999 410 5
Mission Possible, compiled by David Gatward, ISBN 1 85999 411 3
and
Families Finding Faith, by John Hattam, ISBN 1 85999 384 2

Why not ask your church to buy the books and have them available to lend out to any folk who are interested in finding out more?

Top tip

Are there children who used to come along to your *Tiddlywinks* group but who have since grown up and lost touch with the church? Could you send them a special invitation to your church holiday club, mid-week club or Sunday group? You might be able to get back in touch with several families if you hunt out old registers to find their addresses.

ACTIVITY PAGE: Photocopy page 43 for use

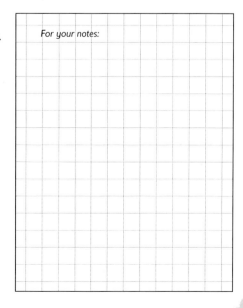

For your notes:

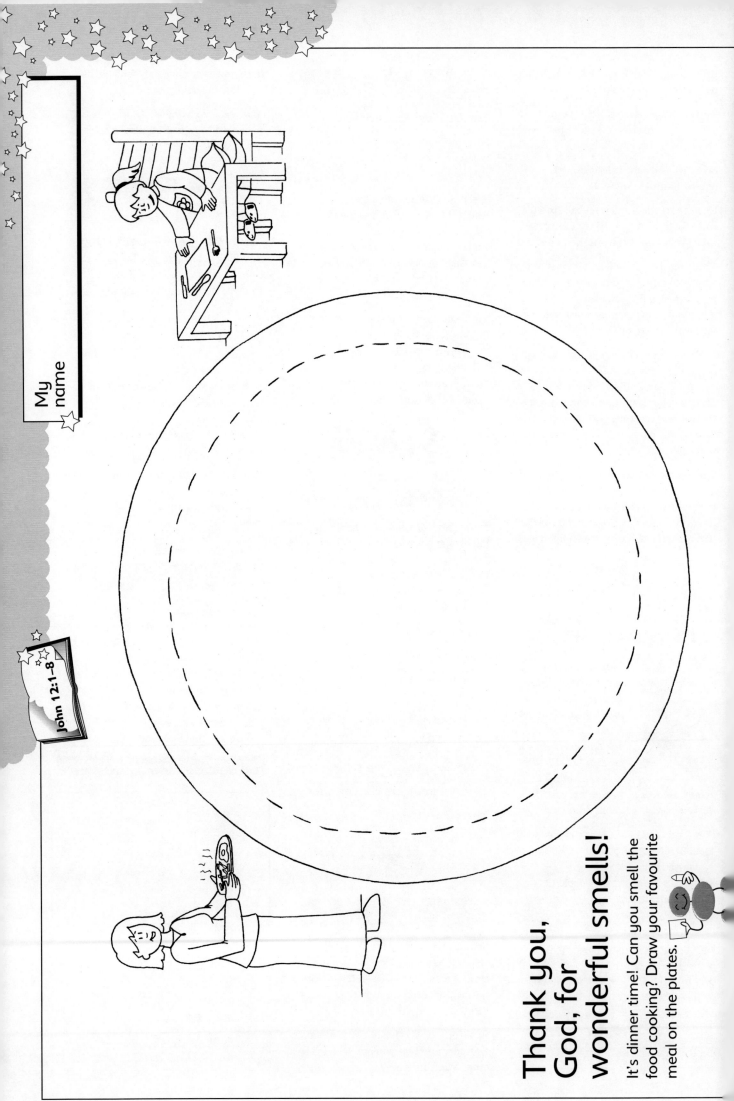

My name

John 12:1-8

Thank you, God, for wonderful smells!

It's dinner time! Can you smell the food cooking? Draw your favourite meal on the plates.

God made me. I'm growing!

Fold 1

Fold 2

My name

1 Samuel 3

Fold the paper in half away from you, along Fold 1. Fold the paper down towards you along Fold 2. How tall is Samuel? Open up the paper. How tall is Samuel now?

B11 God gives us...
Homes to live in
A home for Elisha

2 Kings 4: 8-11

Play time

You will need: building bricks, Duplo, megablocks, empty shoeboxes, large cardboard boxes.

Build it up

Use whatever style building blocks you have access to, eg wooden bricks, *Duplo*, *Megablocks*, and allow the children to have a free playtime in construction. If the children are used to playing with a certain type of block, you may be able to borrow another type for a change. As the children play, talk to them about what they are building, or give them a challenge: 'Can you build a tower as tall as yourself?'

For an added variety in the size of the building materials, you can make some large bricks from empty shoeboxes. Ask your local shoe shop if they can donate some to you. Seal on the lid with tape and cover with coloured paper. You will need twelve or more boxes, depending on your space and number of children.

For an even larger style of building block, ask your local supermarket for some large cardboard boxes and encourage the children to use their imagination to create a space to live in. Some boxes may be big enough for the children to sit in!

The children will enjoy trying out the different variety of materials. Be careful not to build for them. The children will welcome your delight and praise when their construction is complete. Be aware that some children may become upset when their tower falls down. Help them to see that it can be built again.

20-30 mins

Game time

You will need: a soft ball.

Thank you ball

Start by asking the children to form a circle and then to sit down, with their legs stretched in a V in front of them. Sit in the middle of the circle and roll the ball to each child in turn. As the child receives the ball, encourage them to say 'Thank you... *(add your name)*' and roll the ball back to you. As you receive the ball, return the 'Thank you... *(add the child's name)*'. After a while, join the circle and encourage a child to take your place in the middle of the circle. This game encourages the children to be kind to each other as they take turns.

7-10 mins

Making time

You will need: one copy of simple house outline per child, coloured paper or card cut into squares, crayons, sticky tape.

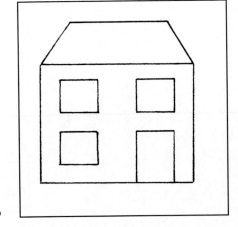

You will need to prepare house outlines for each child. On an A4 sheet of card or paper, draw a simple house outline. Add four square windows, a rectangular door and an additional square window in the roof. Copy enough for each child in your group. From a different colour card, cut enough square shapes to cover the windows or use the designs given here.

Encourage the children to draw members of their family and their friends in each of the windows and then to colour in the front door.

Ask the children how many square windows they can see on their house. Count with them and then distribute the coloured squares. Encourage the children to match the coloured squares to the squares on their house. With a small amount of tape, stick the top side of the coloured square to the house. This will now give a 'lift-the-flap' style picture.

Add the caption: 'Elisha's friends let him stay at their house' at the bottom of the picture.

10-12 mins

Story time

You will need: three play people , eg Duplo, a shoebox (without the lid), scissors, one smaller box which will balance across the top of the shoebox and some doll's house furniture, eg tables, chairs, beds.

Cut windows and a door into the shoebox to make the house. Move the play people in and out of the house as you tell the story.

I'm going to tell you a story from the Bible. A long time ago, before you or I were born, there lived a man *(hold up one of the play people)*. His name was Elisha. Elisha walked from town to town, telling people about God.

In one town, Elisha met a very kind lady *(introduce another play figure to meet Elisha)*. 'Would you like to come and have tea at our house?' she asked him. 'Yes, please!' Elisha replied. They went into the lady's house *(move the figures into the house and add table and three chairs and third play figure)* and sat down to eat. Elisha enjoyed meeting the lady and her husband and sharing a meal with them.

After tea, Elisha was tired and needed to sleep, but the lady's house was very small and there wasn't enough room for Elisha to sleep there.

One day, the lady had a good idea. She said to her husband: 'Let's build another room onto our house for Elisha. We can put a bed, a chair, a table and a lamp in it. Then Elisha can sleep here when he comes to our town.'

(Take the smaller box and balance it on top of the house. Put the lady and husband play figures in it. Then add a bed, a chair and table.) The lady and her husband were very busy making the room strong and comfortable for Elisha, so that whenever he visited their house he could always sleep in his own special room.

Elisha was very happy with his new room (put the Elisha play figure in the smaller box). 'You have been so kind to me,' he said to the lady and her husband. 'Thank you so much!'

After you have told the story, give the children a chance to play out the story again, using the storytelling equipment.

Rhyme time

Who lives in a home like this?
Explain to the children that each verse is about someone's home. Encourage them to listen carefully to each verse and then guess whose home it might be.

My home is very cosy;
It's high up in a tree.
When I look out of my home
The whole town I can see.
Guess who? *(Bird)*

My home is stuck upon me;
It is a great big shell.
I can curl right up inside
If I'm not feeling well.
Guess who? *(Snail)*

My home, when I was born,
Was a stable small and cold.
My bed was the animal's manger;
My blanket was straw, so I'm told.
Guess who? *(Jesus)*

My home has got some bedrooms,
A bathroom, lounge and hall.
My home has got a kitchen;
There's enough room for us all.
Guess who? *(Me)*

Song time

Sing to the tune of 'There was a princess long ago'.

Elisha came a-walking by, walking by,
    walking by, *(walk on the spot)*
Elisha came a-walking by, long, long ago.

A lady said, 'Come in for tea, in for tea,
    in for tea,' *(rub tummy)*
A lady said, 'Come in for tea,'
    long, long ago.

Elisha said, 'I'm very tired, very tired,
    very tired,' *(rub eyes)*
Elisha said, 'I'm very tired,'
    long, long ago.

The lady's house was far too small, far too
    small, far too small, *(crouch down)*
The lady's house was far too small;
    Elisha couldn't stay.

The lady built another room,
    another room, another room
(use hands to make a building action)
The lady built another room;
    Elisha can stay now.

Thank you, God, for giving us,
    giving us, giving us… *(praying hands)*
Thank you God for giving us homes
    where we can live.

Pray time

Prayer Picture
You will need: pictures cut from magazines/estate agents' brochures of a variety of homes, a large sheet of paper, glue sticks, marker pen.

Explain that people all over the world live in many different kinds of homes. Hold up some of the pictures and talk about the different places people live (houses, bungalows, flats, huts, igloos etc).

Invite each child to choose a picture of a home and stick it onto the large sheet of paper. Add the words: 'Thank you, God, for homes to live in' at the top of the collage.

Gather around the prayer picture. Then pray, pointing to and naming each home in turn.

Extra time

 Use the traditional nursery song "London Bridge". Ask the children for suggestions of materials to use to rebuild the bridge.

Sing 'The wise man built his house upon the rock' *KS 336.*

Adults too

Generally, children love their homes and are proud to live in them. As adults, we sometimes worry too much that our homes don't live up to the images we see on TV and in magazines.

Jesus' message to us is that people are more important than material things – which means that the people who live in our homes are more important than the décor and what we own! The time we have for each other and the love we show each other are the most important things to have in our homes.

Top tip

Wooden bricks falling from high towers can be hazardous. Make sure the children have enough space for free playtime. If you cannot play with a variety of building blocks at one time, introduce them separately.

ACTIVITY PAGE: Photocopy page 48 for use

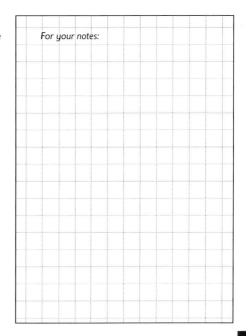

For your notes:

B12 God gives us...
Clothes to wear
Dorcas

Acts 9: 36-40

Play time

You will need: *selection of dressing-up clothes and accessories (hats/scarves/sunglasses/bead necklaces) of different colours and textures.*

Find and feel

Pack your dressing-up kit into a large trunk or box. Gather the children around to find out what is inside. Invite a child to pull something out of the box. Talk to the children about the item, perhaps asking them: 'What do you think this is made from? Who do you think would wear this? When would you wear this?'

Give the children time to look at and handle the garments and accessories. Then encourage them to dress up. Some children may need more encouragement than others, and some may not want to dress up at all but will enjoy watching the others.

Try to bring a mirror so the children can admire their dressing-up experiments. If you are feeling adventurous, join in the dressing-up time. Children enjoy it when we play with them!

Dressing-up clothes do not have to be off-the-peg costumes but can be a variety of borrowed, clean garments. Large, colourful scarves are particularly useful, and can become a range of different outfits. Net curtains can become a wedding veil or a princess skirt. Try to have a selection of hats used for different professions, eg firefighter, police officer, builder. Add a number of accessories and props, eg safe beads, bags, sunglasses and gloves. Cardboard tubes from kitchen rolls make good binoculars or a telescope, and paper plates instantly become steering wheels.

Game time

You will need: *pairs of socks.*

Hunt the Sock

Gather enough pairs of socks (preferably with striking colours and patterns) for each child to find one of a pair. Hide the socks around the room.

Explain to the children that all your socks have gone missing somewhere in the room, and you need the children to help you to find them. Ask them to find one sock each and keep hold of it. Once all the socks have been found, gather the children into a circle. Explain that socks always come in twos. So you need their help to put the socks back in their pairs. Ask the children to look carefully at the sock they are holding and then at the socks everyone else is holding. Can they see the sock that matches the one they are holding? If they can see it, they must go and sit next to the person holding it.

When all the socks are in pairs, gather them up and thank the children for helping you.

Making time

Lacing cards
You will need: *coloured wool, clear sticky tape, large pictures cut from old greetings cards, hole-punch.*

Cut large, simple pictures (teddy bears, rockets, flowers) from old birthday cards. Alternatively, draw a simple outline of a teddy bear or car onto coloured card (see this page). Loosely cut the picture from the card and make holes around the outside of the picture using a hole-punch. Younger children will only be able to manage a few holes; older children will be able to do more. Make sure you have a card outline for each child.

Cut lengths of wool and seal the ends with clear tape. This makes it easier for the children to thread the wool through the holes.

Tape one end of the wool to the card. The children then 'sew' around the edge of the card. When they have finished, secure the other end of the wool onto the back of the card with sticky tape.

An adult will need to supervise this activity all the time. Younger children will need one-to-one attention.

Story time

You will need: *a large shawl, a shirt, two pieces of fabric with needle and thread, a few small items of children's clothing, a large box or basket.*

Pack all the items into the box or basket beforehand. Bring out your box and explain to the children that it is a story box. Inside it there are lots of things to help you tell a story from the Bible. Explain that you are going to pretend to be a lady called Dorcas, and the children can join in and pretend to be her friends.

Long ago, before you and I were born, a lady named Dorcas lived in a town called Joppa. *(Take the shawl from your story box and wrap it around your shoulders, to dress as Dorcas.)*

Dorcas was very clever. She could make clothes. *(Take out the shirt and hold it up for the children to see.)*

Dorcas could cut material into different shapes and sew them together to make things like dresses and shirts. *(Demonstrate sewing the two pieces of material together as you tell this part of the story.)*

Dorcas was a friend of Jesus, and she

always remembered how Jesus taught people to be kind and to help one another. So, Dorcas used her special gift of making clothes to help other people who lived in Joppa.

Some people didn't have enough money to buy new clothes for themselves or their children, and so Dorcas would make some for them. *(Take from the story box a few items of clothing and hand them out to some of the children.)*

The people in Joppa loved Dorcas because she was so kind.

Ask the children to help you to re-pack the story box. Make a point of putting the needle and thread away very carefully. Thank them for their help.

Rhyme time

Clothes for every Season
You will need: a raincoat, a sun hat, a pair of trousers, a scarf.

In the spring, when it showers with rain,
We wear our raincoats 'til the
  sun comes again. *(Put on raincoat.)*
In summer, the sun shines hot
  while we play;
Shorts and a sun hat keep us
  cool all day. *(Put on sun hat.)*
In autumn, when leaves gently
  fall from the trees,
We need long trousers that
  cover our knees. *(Hold up trousers.)*
Winter brings cold winds and
  ice on the path;
So we wear woolly jumpers,
  hats and scarves. *(Put on scarf.)*
God gives us clothes for all that we do,
For he loves and he cares
  for me and for you.

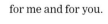

Song time

Explain to the children that they are going to pretend to be Dorcas as they sing this song to the tune of 'Twinkle, twinkle little star'.

Stitching, stitching all day long,
(use hand in sewing action)

Making clothes for everyone.
One stitch here and one stitch there
(count, using fingers)
My friends need new clothes to wear.
Jesus says be kind to others,
(point and look upwards)
Parents, friends, sisters and brothers.
(Point round the circle to each other.)

Pray time

You will need: string or rope, coloured paper cut in shape of T-shirt, crayons, pegs (coloured, if possible).

Washing line prayer.
Make a washing line with the string across the room. Make sure it is low enough for the children to reach. (Washing lines can be dangerous for young children running around, so put up your washing line just before you pray.)

Explain to the children that today you are going to make prayers to God together.

Give each child a paper T-shirt shape. Ask the children if they have a favourite dress or jumper etc; encourage them to draw it on their paper shape. When they have finished, distribute coloured pegs to the children and help them to peg their prayer onto the line.

As you peg the T-shirt on, say: "Thank you, God, for my… Amen."

Extra time

•Let the children tear (or cut) pictures of clothes from magazines. Stick them on paper to make a collage.

•Suitable books to read are:
The Emperor's New Clothes (traditional)
Alfie's Feet by Shirley Hughes (Collins, ISBN 0 00 662161 9)
Postman Pat's Washing Day by John Cunliffe
(André Deutsch, ISBN 0233 98297 3)
All in One Piece by Jill Murphy (Walker Books, ISBN 0 7445 0749 9)
You'll Soon Grow into there, Titch by Pat Hutchins (Red Fox ISBN 0099 20711 7).

Adults too

We all have a special gift – sometimes it takes another person to help us to recognise what it is. As Christians, we believe that we use the gift that God has given us to help others. You may like to encourage the adults to think about the gifts that they have and how they could use them to assist one another, eg cake decorating, DIY skills, hairdressing, computing skills.

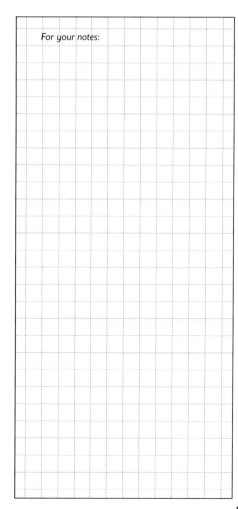

If some of the parents and carers are good at organising events, why not stage a Talent Auction, where people offer their skills and others bid for them, as a fundraising event?

ACTIVITY PAGE: Photocopy page 49 for use

For your notes:

2 Kings 4: 8-11

God gives me my home.

Here is Elisha's new room with the table and the lamp. But where are his bed and his chair? Draw a bed and a chair for Elisha.

God gives me clothes to wear.

Dorcas made clothes for her friends.
Draw the clothes that Dorcas made on these people.

Acts 9:
36-40

B13 God gives us...
Food to eat

God gives us the food we need

Exodus 13: 3-10; Exodus 16

Play time

You will need: *play cooker, small tables, toy teaset and saucepans, paper or plastic plates, toy or plastic cutlery and utensils, toy play food, play dough, rolling-pins and cutters, aprons, recipe books, small tablecloths, paper napkins.*

Have a selection of free-play activities set out for the children. Create a 'kitchen corner'. If you have access to a play cooker, make this the main focus. Alternatively, create a cooker using a large cardboard box. Stick on black circles for the hob and add washing detergent bottle tops for knobs.

Set out a table for 'food preparation' and for serving up the finished products. Provide aprons, play dough, rolling-pins and cutters, and encourage the children to prepare and cook for each other. Look through some recipe books together. As the children play, talk with them about their favourite food and your favourite food.

In another corner, create an eating area. Encourage the children to lay the table, using cloths, play crockery and cutlery. Divide the play food between the two areas.

Don't forget to 'eat' the food they cook for you and help with the washing up!

Toy microwaves, toasters, and play food with halves joined by hook and loop fasteners to make it easy to cut are all available commercially. You may be able to borrow play equipment from another local group or toy library. It is worth building up your 'kitchen' corner over time, investing in good play equipment.

Game time

Sensory Foods
You will need: *five empty ice-cream containers (without lids), fabric, grapes, mature cheese, uncooked rice, chocolate buttons, crisps, elastic bands, a bowl of water and towel.*

Cut four pieces of fabric to fit over the top of the containers. Three pieces of fabric will need a slit cut for the children to reach inside the container. Place the food in different containers. Then attach the fabric to each container with a large elastic band.

Explain to the children that this game is all about using our senses, touching, smelling, hearing, tasting and looking to recognise different foods. Reassure them that there is nothing horrible in the containers!

Container 1
A bunch of grapes
Touch and feel what's in the box, then guess what it is.

Container 2
Strong cheese.
Can they guess by smelling?

Container 3
Dried rice.
Shake the box. What could make that noise?

Container 4
Chocolate buttons.
Close your eyes, reach into the box, take whatever is inside and taste it. Can they guess what it is?

Container 5
Crisps.
Look inside together. What do you see? Let them share the crisps.

Provide a bowl of water and a towel to wash the children's hands afterwards.

Making time

Grace plate
You will need: *large paper plates (one for each child), pictures of food, glue sticks, a marker pen.*

Cut out plenty of pictures of food from magazines [TIP: many supermarkets give away free monthly magazines and leaflets]. It is a good idea to have a few of the same picture, especially for popular favourites like fish fingers and ice-cream. Write a simple grace on the back of each plate, eg 'Dear God, thank you for giving us food to eat. Amen.'

The children choose a selection of food pictures to make a 'meal' and stick them onto their plate. As the children finish their collage, turn the plate over and read the prayer to the child.

The children can take the grace plate home to use at meal times with their family.

Story time

You will need: *a potato, a parsnip, wool, coloured paper, red felt (optional), pitta bread, frosted cereal flakes.*

The characters in the story are created using vegetables as puppets. Use a potato for Sam and a small parsnip for Sarah. Make eyes from coloured paper and attach wool for hair and red felt (or paper) for a mouth. Use the floor or a low table for your stage, and move the characters around as two leaders tell the story – one narrating and one taking on the character voices.

Narrator: A long time ago, before you or I were born, in a country called Egypt lived Sam and Sarah.

Sam: Mmmmmmmm – what's that lovely smell?

Sarah: Mmmmmmmm – I smell bread.

Narrator: Sam and Sarah's mummy was baking bread in the kitchen. Mummy put the bread on a plate and gave it to Sam and Sarah. (Add a plate with pitta bread to the scene.)

Sam: This bread looks different. It looks flat.

Narrator: Sam and Sarah's mummy said that they were to eat the bread up quickly because they were moving to a new place to live. God had told her to make this special bread but not let it rise up into a big loaf.

Sam and Sarah started to eat the flat bread. *(Invite the children to share the bread with Sam and Sarah.)* Then they started on the journey to their new home.

Sam: It hasn't been much fun living in Egypt.

Sarah: God is helping us to move to a new place where we shall be happy again.

Narrator: On the way, they stopped to camp in the desert. Sam soon started to complain.

Sam: I'm really hungry. My tummy's rumbling.

Narrator: Mummy said she hadn't got anything to eat but she would ask their friend Moses, who was travelling too. Moses told everybody to remember that God was looking after them and would give them food in the morning.

When Sam woke up next morning, he was very excited.

Sam: Look, God has sent us food.

Narrator: The ground was covered with crispy, white flakes.

Sarah: Can we eat it now?

Narrator: Sam and Sarah collected the flakes. (Add a bowl of frosted cereal to the scene.) Sam and Sarah liked the food. It was called 'manna' and tasted very sweet.

(Let the children share the 'manna'.)

Every day of the journey to their new home, God gave Sam, Sarah and their family manna to eat.

Sam: Thank you, God – I'm not hungry now.

Sarah: Thank you, God, for giving us just what we need.

Rhyme time

'How does God give me my tea?'
I heard a small boy say.
His mummy smiled and then she said:
'It happens just this way:
God helps farmers work so hard
    to grow the food we eat –
Corn for bread, fruit for pies,
    vegetables and beet.
God helps fishermen to catch fish
    from the great big sea,
Sardines on toast, tuna rolls or cod
    with chips – yummy!
God helps those who work in shops
    and market stalls as well –
Butchers, bakers and greengrocers –

all with food to sell.
God helps those who buy the food and
    cook it, just like me,
So you see, my little one, how
    God gives you your tea!'

Song time

Change 'The farmer's in his den' to the following words:

Mummy's making bread, *(stirring action)*
Mummy's making bread,
We can all smell the bread, *(touch nose)*
Mummy's making bread.
The bread it must not rise, *(shake head)*
The bread it must not rise,
Mummy heard God speak, he said
    (cup hand behind ear)
The bread it must not rise.
The bread is very flat, *(clap hands)*
The bread is very flat.
We can all touch the bread,
    (stroke palm of hand)
The bread is very flat.
Hurry, eat the bread, *(eating action)*
Hurry, eat the bread,
We can all taste the bread, *(touch lips)*
Hurry eat the bread.
God cares for all of us,
    (hold hands and swing arms)
God cares for all of us,
God gives us all our bread each day,
God cares for all of us.

Pray time

Ask the children and the grown-ups what their favourite food is. Say the following response prayer and weave in some of the food suggested by the group.

Encourage everyone to join in with 'God gives us the food we need'. Finish with a rousing 'Amen' and give God a big clap to say thank you.

Toast with *Marmite* or with jam
God gives us the food we need.

Ham sandwiches with cucumber in
God gives us the food we need.

Apples, bananas and satsumas in juice
God gives us the food we need.

Chicken nuggets with baked beans and chips

God gives us the food we need.

Food to help us grow healthy and strong
God gives us the food we need.

Thank you, Father God, for giving us all we need. Amen

Extra time

• Sing 'Five currant buns in the baker's shop…' using the names of children in your group.

• The traditional rhyme 'Pat-a-cake, Pat-a-cake, baker man' can be used if adults are present with their small children. Older children can divide into pairs and use this rhyme as a clapping game together.

Adults too

Maybe the adults who come along to your group are not used to praying at home. Why not set out a selection of prayer books for adults and children and encourage the adults to browse through them over coffee? Set up a library system so that carers can borrow the books. Alternatively, find out whether your local Christian bookshop can provide books on a sale or return basis. Introduce the book selection by saying that one way of remembering God's care for us every day is to pause before we eat our food and thank him for all we have to eat. Once this habit is established, you will probably find that your children want to 'say grace' for everyone.

Top tip

Home-made play dough is cheap and easy to make. You will need: 2 cups plain flour; 1 cup salt; 2 cups water; 2 tablespoons oil; 2 teaspoons cream of tartar; a few drops of food colouring. Mix all ingredients in a heavy saucepan. Cook over a medium heat, stirring all the time. Remove from heat when mixture comes away from the sides of the pan. Knead into dough when cool enough to touch.

For a no-cook salt dough recipe, see Session 8 'I can make'.

ACTIVITY PAGE: Photocopy page 54 for use

B14 God gives us...
Parties to enjoy
The great feast

Luke 14: 15-24

Play time

You will need: *balloons, party music, play food, play dough, party paper plates and cups, wrapping paper or crêpe paper, round-ended scissors, sticky tape, dressing-up clothes and accessories, bubble mixture and bubble blower sticks.*

Party time

Before the children arrive, hang some balloons as decorations and select some party music on CD/cassette. Play the music quietly as the children arrive. Set out various free-play activities designed to create a party atmosphere.

Party food

Arrange a kitchen corner where the children can make platefuls of party-style food with play food and play dough. Encourage them to prepare a party table with a party cloth, paper plates and plastic cups. While they play, talk to them about the sort of food they like to eat at parties. Don't forget to join them at the party table when the play food is ready!

Party decorations

Set aside a table to make decorations. Cut strips of wrapping paper (these can be prepared beforehand) and assist the children in making paper chains to decorate the room.

Party clothes

Fancy dress always adds colour to a party, so let the children loose on the dressing-up box.

Party bubbles

The children can chase, pop and help you to blow bubbles. Shop-bought bubble mixture is quite inexpensive, or you can make your own (see Top Tip).

Party games

Complete your party playtime with a couple of circle games, such as 'Ring a ring of roses' and the 'Hokey Cokey'.

no limit

Game time

You will need: *old greetings cards (birthday, Christmas, anniversary, wedding etc).*

Allow one card for each child in your group. Using the picture sides of the card only, cut them in half. Place one half of the pictures around the room (remember to keep them at child height). Distribute the remaining halves of the cards to the children. Ask them to look very carefully at their piece of card and then 'hunt' around the room for the other half. Very young children will need one-to-one help from the adults in the group. When the children have two halves, they are to come to show you their complete card.

7 mins

Making time

Feasty Fancies

You will need: *round, plain biscuits (at least one per child), aprons, icing sugar, teaspoons, treats for decorating (chocolate buttons, sugar flowers, silver balls etc), cake cases, greaseproof paper.* ***Safety note:*** *Remember to check whether any children have any food allergies and make sure that you adhere to food preparation hygiene requirements.*

Set up a table with a few bowls of white icing (made to a consistency that will run off a spoon) and a number of teaspoons. When the children have washed their hands and put on aprons, seat them around the clean working surface and distribute the biscuits and treats. Avoid squabbles by giving each child a cake case with a few decorating treats in it. Explain to the children to keep their hands out of their mouths while they are 'cooking'. Show them how to put a little icing on the biscuit with a teaspoon. Younger children may need an adult to help with this. Let them decorate the iced biscuit as they wish. [TIP: keep some 'spare' treats, in case some are eaten before they reach the biscuit!]

Place biscuits on greaseproof paper marked with the child's name. The biscuits will set during the session and can be taken home wrapped in the greaseproof paper.

5-8 mins

Story time

You will need: *tambourine, shakers, kazoo, bells, wood block.*

The different instruments represent characters in the story. A leader who is not the storyteller is also needed to operate the wood block. Set the instruments on a small table or tray, out of reach of the children. Tell the children that there are all sorts of people in your story today; each one has a special sound. There is a rich man (shake tambourine), an old man (shakers), a woman (kazoo) and a young man (bells). Ask them to listen out for the sound of someone knocking at the door (wood block).

A long time ago, before you and I were born, Jesus was at a party. In the middle of the party, Jesus told this story.

Once upon a time there was a rich man who decided to have a party *(tambourine)*.

He got everything ready for the party – the decorations, the food, the drinks and the games.

Then he told his servant to go and invite some people from the town.

The servant knocked at the first door *(wood block)*.

An old man came to the door *(shakers)*: 'I can't come to the party – I've got to look after my garden!' *(Shakers.)*

The servant knocked at the next door *(wood block)*.

A woman came to the door (kazoo): 'I can't come to the party – I've got to look after my cow!' *(Kazoo.)*

The servant knocked at the next door *(wood block)*.

A young man came to the door *(bells)*: 'I can't come to the party; I've got to look after my wife!' (Bells.)

The servant went back to the rich man (tambourine) and told him that nobody could come to the party. The rich man was cross (tambourine). He said: 'Go back into the town and ask all the poor people, all the sick people, and all the blind people who live in this town. Nobody ever invites them, but I want them to come to my party!' (Tambourine.)

The servant went back and knocked on all the doors (wood block). And all the people came. (Hand the instruments out to children in the group.) It was the best party ever. (Play all the instruments together.)

Rhyme time

Repeat the rhyme a few times and encourage the children to join in.

We've lots of food and games to play…
(Clap) Let's have a party!
Invite the guests to come and stay…
(Clap) Let's have a party!
The guests say, 'I can't come today!'
Ohhhhhh! (Make a sad face.)
We'll ask more folk to join the fun…
(Clap) Let's have a party!
There's lots of room for everyone…
We're having a party! (Wave arms in air.)
Hooray! (Cheer and clap.)

Song time

Divide into two groups and sing the following words to the tune of 'Frère Jacques':

Group one:
There's a party, there's a party
In the town, in the town.
Hurry, you're invited!
Hurry, you're invited!
Lots of fun for everyone.

Group two:
There's a party, there's a party
In the town, in the town.
Sorry, we're too busy!
Sorry, we're too busy!

We can't come. We can't come.

Group one:
(Repeats first verse.)

Group two:
There's a party, there's a party
In the town, in the town.
Thank you, we are coming.
Thank you, we are coming.
God's love is for everyone.

Pray time

Beforehand, inflate enough balloons for each child in your group. With a permanent marker write one party 'Thank you' on each balloon, eg 'Thank you God for music' or 'Thank you God for yummy food.'

Gather the children into a standing circle. Explain that we are going to talk to God and say thank you to him for giving us parties to enjoy.

Distribute the balloons, asking the children to hold on to them carefully. Explain that their balloon has a special thank you to God written on it. Ask the adults in your group to read the thank you to the children.

As you pray the Thank You prayer the children can throw their balloons up in the air (repeatedly). Finish the prayer with an 'Amen' together.

Extra time

•Make simple party hats. Provide crayons and/or shapes cut from gummed paper, and let the children make colourful creations.

•Play traditional party and singing games, eg Simon says, Musical bumps, Pass the parcel

Adults too

If your group draws in adults and children from your community who do not come to worship on Sundays, it may be that they are just waiting for an invitation to come along. Some people find it easier to come along to a church service for the first time if they have been personally invited. Give out party-style invitations to the adults to come along to the next family service or festival service. Include on the invitation any information about the Sunday children's groups, and aim to help them feel comfortable and welcome.

Top tip

Bubble mixture
Use bubble bath mixture or good quality washing-up liquid. Mix half a cup with one-third of a cup of water in a basin. Make bubble blowers from twisted wire loops. Square or triangular shaped blowers make interesting bubbles. Set up the bubble blowing activity in an area where the floor will not get slippery if bubble mixture drips on to it.

ACTIVITY PAGE: Photocopy page 55 for use

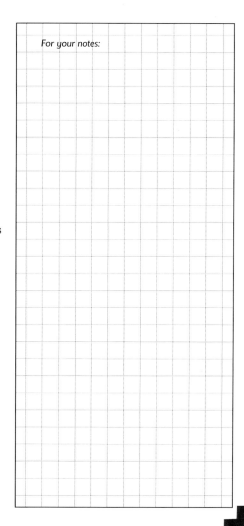

For your notes:

My name

Exodus 13:
3-10;
Exodus 16

God gives me food to eat.

Find the same food. Look at the first picture in each row. Can you find another picture exactly the same? Colour in the matching food pictures.

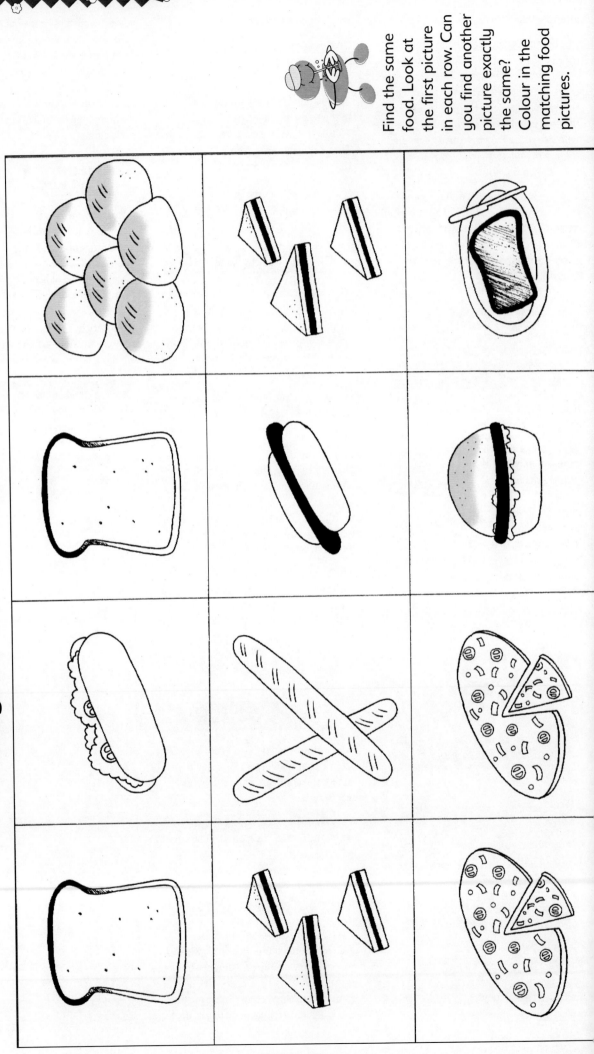

My name

Luke 14:
15-24

Thank you, God, for parties.

A man had a party. He asked some people to come but they said "no". So he asked all the poor and ill people to come. Put a tick by the people who went to the party.

55

B15 God gives us...
Holidays to have fun

God's day to rest

Genesis 2: 1-3

Play time

You will need: *play sand, sand tray, small buckets, spades, rakes (if these are not available, use large yoghurt pots, spoons and large combs), funnels, sea shells, empty plastic containers, a tray, a beach ball.*

Set up various free-play activities to create a seaside holiday feel.

Sand play

If you do not have access to a nursery water or sand tray, an old baby bath or large washing-up bowl works just as well to contain sand for play. Play sand can be purchased from DIY outlets or stores selling children's play equipment. Children love playing with sand, so if your group is large you may need to provide more than one sand container, to give the children plenty of space to play. Provide small buckets, spades and rakes. Instead of buckets and spades, you could use large, empty yoghurt pots and spoons. Large combs make excellent rakes. Although the sand areas will need to be closely supervised, allow free play for the children to discover and explore the properties of the sand. The children will enjoy pouring and filling the containers – plastic funnels add

to this fun. Encourage the children to build simple sandcastles (you will need to dampen the sand first).

Flying flags

Set up an area for the children to make simple flags to decorate the sandcastles. Cut triangles from coloured paper and attach them with sticky tape or staples to a drinking straw.

Sorting shells

Clean seaside shells of various sizes and textures are fun to explore. Lay them out on a tray and provide some empty containers for children to use to sort and shake the shells. Help the children to form pictures using the shells on the empty tray.

Bouncing balls

If you have the space, introduce an inflatable beach ball or two and allow the children time to throw, roll and chase the ball together.

no limit

Game time

Bucket that ball

You will need: *a large seaside bucket, a long-handled spade and a small, soft ball (the ones made out of foam work well).*

This is a game of skill and balance. The idea is that the children will take turns to walk, from a starting point, balancing a ball on the spade. The seaside bucket will be placed at a finishing point and when the child arrives the ball is tipped into the bucket. If the ball is dropped on the way to the bucket, the child returns to the starting point to have another go.

At every successful deposit into the bucket, the rest of the children are encouraged to give a loud cheer of praise.

If you are working with a large group of children, you may need two groups playing at the same time. However, there is no competitive element to the game.

7-10 mins

Making time

The idea here is for the children to enjoy free time for personal creativity.

Provide each child with a large sheet of paper, pre-printed with 'God gives *(child's name)* time to have fun.'

Provide a variety of media for creative art: collage materials, glue, crayons, paint. (This is a good way to use up bits and bobs from your resource cupboard). Allow the children the freedom to make whatever they like. Alternatively, suggest

that they make something to show what God created in his wonderful world, ie an animal, a bird, a tree or plant or some people.

Give this activity a set time and then spend time together showing and telling about the work. Ask the children if they enjoyed making it and are they pleased with it? Remind them that just as we like making things, God liked making the world for us to live in and he was very pleased with the world that he created. He loves us very much.

If 'Making time' comes after 'Story time,' you may find some work is as a response to the story.

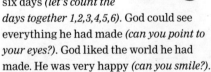
10-15 mins

Story time

Response Story

Invite the children to join you to sit on the story mat. You may like to use a large picnic blanket. Explain that you need help to tell today's story and the children can help you by joining in some actions to special words in the story. They will have to listen very carefully to hear the special words.

A very long time ago, before you or I were born, God was busy making the whole world. God worked for six days *(let's count the days together 1,2,3,4,5,6)*. God could see everything he had made *(can you point to your eyes?)*. God liked the world he had made. He was very happy *(can you smile?)*.

God said 'I've worked for six days' *(count the days together 1,2,3,4,5,6)*. God said 'I can see everything I have made' *(point to eyes)*. God said 'I like it very much. I am very happy' *(smile)*.

So, on the next day, the seventh day *(count the days together 1,2,3,4,5,6,7)* God had finished making the world *(let's give God a clap and shout 'Hoorah!')*.

God said 'Today is the seventh day' *(count the days together 1,2,3,4,5,6,7)*. 'I have finished making the world *(make a circle with your arms to show the world)* and it is very good' *(Clap and shout 'Hoorah!'z)*

God said 'Today is a special day.' He took a break from making things and spent his time enjoying all the beautiful things that he had made in his world *(make a circle with your arms)*.

I wonder what He did? *(the children may have some suggestions here)*

What do you like to do when you have a day off from going to nursery or when you go on holiday?

Rhyme time

The Days of My Week
On Monday I go swimming.
On Tuesday I shop with Mum.
On Wednesday and Thursday
it's Pre-school,
And on Friday Grandma comes.
On Saturday there're jobs to do:
We wash and dust and bake;
There's grass to mow, the car to clean
And all the beds to make.
But Sunday is quite different:
It's God's special day, you see;
One day out of seven
That he made for you and me.
God took a rest on Sunday
When the world was all complete.
So we should do that too, you see,
Sit down and rest our feet.

Do any of the children do these things? What day is it today? What normally happens today?

Song time

Holidays are lots of fun
(Tune: 'Heads, shoulders, knees and toes')

Holidays are lots of fun, lots of fun
When we're playing in the sun,
    in the sun, so,
Thank you, God, for all our holidays.
We can have a happy time.

This song works well with the children playing percussion accompaniment on shakers.

You can also sing about the things we can do whilst enjoying our holidays.

Choose familiar songs, such as: 'Row, row, row your boat' – with this additional verse:

Row, row, row your boat

Gently down the stream.
When we are on holiday
We like to eat ice-cream. *(Yum, yum, yum!)*

Pray time

Reflect with the children on how busy they have been, and that we are now going to rest with God. God knows that when we have been busy it is then important to have a rest. That is what God did when he finished making the world.

Invite the children to find a space, lie down and be very still by the time you have counted (slowly) to three.

Explain to the children that together we shall talk quietly to God – ask the children to repeat what you say in a whisper:

Dear Father God,
Thank you for making our world.
We can have fun in our world.
We can rest in our world.
Thank you for making our world.
Amen.

Now the children can quietly and slowly sit up, to the count of three again.

Extra time

Go into your local travel agent and pick up a few holiday brochures. Try to choose ones that will have a variety of locations, eg beaches, countryside, mountains, camping, skiing. Find pictures of people relaxing and resting on their holiday. As the children look through them, talk about holidays, or what things are fun to do. Reinforce that holidays are for 'taking time out' of work – and that is important for everyone.

Adults too

For all of us, life can be hectic – rushing from one thing to the next and juggling family life. It's so important to build in some time to rest. God set us an example by creating a rest day. Jesus knew how important it was to 'take time out' and

---

spend it with his Father (Mark 6: 31–32), even if it was only for a short time during a busy day. Think about how you could create some 'sacred space' for the adults who come along to your group.

Top tip

It's always a good idea to have a few basic rules in place when playing with sand.

1 We keep sand away from each other's eyes.

2 We keep sand away from our mouths. (It tastes YUK!)

3 We have a cleaning up time, and we all join in.

Remind the children of the playing safely rules before you begin.

ACTIVITY PAGE: Photocopy page 60 for use

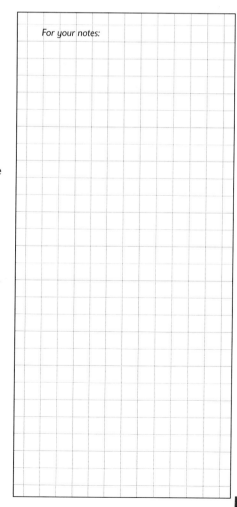

For your notes:

Four fishermen

Matthew 4:18–22

Play time

You will need: *several large cardboard boxes, big enough for children to sit in!*

Make some cardboard fish - the children could help to cut these out and decorate them with glitter glue or shiny paper. Get each child to sit in their fishing boat (a large cardboard box) and spread the fish on the floor around them. Get them to catch as many fish as they can, either with fishing rods made from canes and string with magnets on the end (put a paper clip on the fish to attract the magnet) or nets. If you have some large sheets of bubble wrap, this is good fun to put down (tape to the floor if you'd like it to be fixed more securely) under the boats to create the effect of water.

In addition you could have a plastic fishing set in a water tray to allow more fishing to take place. (Try the Early Learning Centre for one of these.)

Alongside these free play activities, have a largish fish tank or bowl with a selection of objects to allow children to investigate floating and sinking.

 20 mins

Game time

Happy Families
You will need: *several sets of Happy Family cards (use the template on this page) or shop-bought Happy Family playing cards.*

Enlarge the template to make family sets by colouring in the shape people families' clothes in different colours. You can either collect one of each shape to make a family; or collect four of the same shape. (You can easily make larger or smaller families by varying the number of cards in the game.)

Divide the children into small groups of four, with a couple of adults to help. Distribute the cards. Depending on the age and ability of the children, play in the traditional manner, or use cards to play 'Pairs' (spread the cards face down; children take turns to turn over two cards from the table. The aim is to find a pair). Alternatively, play a game of 'snap', or simply arrange the cards in matching families.

 5 mins

Making time

Making disciples
You will need: *large pieces of paper (wallpaper lining rolls work well), aprons, paints, brushes or sponges.*

Ask a child to lie down on a large sheet of paper and draw round them. Draw four figures in this way. Explain that each of the figures is one of Jesus' friends. Provide children with aprons and ask them to paint the figures to make a large display showing the four first disciples. Don't worry about trying to paint on 'biblical' clothing – copying what the children are wearing will be fine! Add the disciple's name next to each figure.

If time is short, just paint two figures for Peter and Andrew, and add the others whenever possible during later sessions.

 10-15 mins

Story time

You will need: *a fishing net (garden pea nets work well).*

Organise beforehand for one of the other leaders to interrupt the story just as you are beginning, by running on with the net, shouting: 'Aha, got you!' and trying to bundle you up in the net. Shout, protest and ask what is going on. The 'fisherman' will explain that Jesus has told him to go out and fish for people, so that is what he is doing. He should look quite indignant that this is not understood but keep smiling so that the children do not get distressed.

Free yourself from the net and ask the 'fisherman' to sit down quietly with the

children and listen: 'I don't think Jesus actually meant to go out and catch real men in your smelly fishing net. Sit down with the children and I'll tell you the story…'

Jesus was walking along the shore of Lake Galilee. He needed some hard-working people who would help him do his work. He saw Peter and Andrew, who were brothers. They were fishermen, and they were mending their nets.

'Leave your nets and come and follow me,' Jesus said. 'I've got a more important job for you to do.'

Peter and Andrew went with Jesus. He wanted them to help him tell people about God, his Father. As they were walking together, they saw James and John, who were also fishermen. Jesus asked them to leave their nets and help him, too: 'I want you to fish for men instead of fish,' he said. So James and John went with him too. Jesus needed lots of people who would help him tell people about God, his Father.

(The 'fisherman' interrupts with: 'So that's what Jesus was talking about!')

Yes, he wants all of us to help him tell other people about God.

Rhyme time

Say this rhyme in the style of: 'One day I went to market'.

First child: Jesus went out to walk one day and he called Andrew to follow him.
Second child: Jesus went out to walk one day and he called Andrew and Peter to follow him etc.

Continue in this way, adding the names of Jesus' friends/helpers each time. Help out those children who struggle to remember a new name. When all the names that you've learned so far have been used, encourage the children to add a name of a child in the group. Don't let the list become too long before starting with one name again.

Song time

'One Elephant' *(Okki-tokki-unga,* A&C Black, London. ISBN 0 7136 4078 2) 'Jesus is the best friend' (67, *GTB,* SU) '1,2,3,4,5 – once I caught a fish alive' and 'Tommy Thumb'.

Sing Tommy Thumb as normal, ie 'Tommy Thumb, Tommy Thumb, where are you? Here I am, here I am, how do you do? At the end of calling for all the fingers (Peter Pointer, Policeman Tall, Ruby Ring, Baby Small), sing out children's names and ask them to answer in the style of the song:

All: Jenny Wren, Jenny Wren, where are you?

JW: Here I am, here I am, how do you do?

Pray time

Find a friend
You will need: *music, eg tape or /CD of children's praise songs.*

Work in a fairly large, clear space. Play some music and ask the children to dance, jump, or move in any way. Stop the music after a short time. When the music stops, ask the children to get into groups of three or four and hold hands in a small circle. Depending on their age and ability, children will need adult help to do this. Once the children are in the groups, invite one child at a time to shout out: 'Thank you, God, for my friend…' (filling in a name of a friend in that group). Just ask two or three children. Then play the music again and repeat the activity in the new groups.

Extra time

•Chat with the children about their friends. Ask each child to name a special friend and say one thing they like about their friend. Adults could start the ball rolling with comments such as: 'Julie is my friend. I like her because she is always smiling,' or: 'I like Jenny because she is kind to me.'

•Read stories about friendships: *Kipper's Birthday,* by Mick Inkpen (Hodder Children's Books) or *Old Bear,* by Jane Hissey (Red Fox); or stories about how we can all play a part and be important: *A duck so small,* by Elisabeth Holstein (Magi Books)

Adults too

Organise a coffee afternoon or evening, or a jewellery/cosmetics party. Invite the parents/carers, so you can get to know each other in a different setting. Invite some of your other friends along, too.

Top tip

During 'Making time', help younger/less able children by painting a thick outline round each area to be painted. Then ask them to paint inside the lines without crossing over them. Remember to provide aprons for this and other messy activities! Don't use ready-pasted wallpaper for this activity. It is hard to paint on and the paste may contain toxic fungicide.

ACTIVITY PAGE: Photocopy page 61 for use

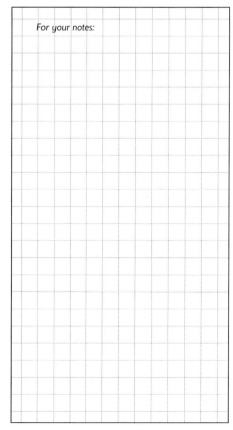

For your notes:

My name

Genesis 2:1–3

Thank you, God, for holidays.

Molly's friends are on holiday and they have each sent her a postcard. Who sent each card? Draw a line from the postcard to the person you think posted it to Molly.

My name

Thank you, God, for our friends.

The friends are busy playing at Nursery. What are they doing today?

Matthew 4:18-22

Count how many

boat

brush

book

car

61

A soldier and a servant

Luke 7: 1–10

Play time

The theme for this session is how much Jesus cares about us, how important it is that we care for one another, especially when someone is ill and how good it is to be cared for when we are ill ourselves.

Set up a hospital/clinic for a role-play area.

You will need: *small blue or white shirts, white aprons, play telephone (or real telephone, if it is disconnected!), pens, notepads, bandages (or strips of paper towel), sticking plasters, latex gloves, walking sticks, toy first aid/doctor's kit, pillows, blankets, dolls and soft toys, ride-on toys.*

Set up a waiting area, with a row of chairs and some books to look at.

Have a receptionist's desk, with telephone, pens and notepads and an appointment book.

Provide small white or blue shirts for doctors and porters, and white aprons and a white card headband with a red cross drawn on for nurses. Have a selection of bandages, sticking plasters, latex gloves, and walking sticks etc. If you have a pretend first aid/doctor's kit, use this as well.

Make up some 'beds' with blankets/quilts and pillows on the floor. Provide some dolls and soft toys to be patients, as well as those children who want to be 'ill'. Ride-on toys can become ambulances, taking the dolls to hospital.

Play alongside the children, talking about how to care for the sick and encouraging appropriate role-play. If the opportunity arises, and it is appropriate, you could pray for the patients.

Game time

People beetle
You will need: *different coloured card, a dice*

Photocopy a simple human body shape onto card and cut into six. Number the pieces from 1-6. Do this on four different coloured pieces of card so that you end up with four separate sets of people pieces (a maximum of four children may play this at the same time). Put all the pieces into the middle of the table. Each child takes it in turns to throw a dice and may collect the body part with the corresponding number (allow each child to collect only one colour). When they throw the dice, if they already have the piece that corresponds to that number, they must miss a go. The winner is the child who completes a whole person first.

 5 mins

Making time

Get well cards
You will need: *thin pieces of sponge, paint trays (meat tins work well), paint, large sheets of paper, thin card.*

Put some thin pieces of sponge into large paint trays (or washed meat tins). Pour in some paint and spread over the surface of the sponge. Invite the children to press their hand into the sponge and have a go at hand printing. Allow the children to print freely on large pieces of paper first; then ask each child to make two hand prints on the front of a card. When dry, the message 'Get well soon' can be written inside by an adult or the child. (See 'Top tip'.)

If a member of the group is ill, or the child knows someone who is ill, these cards can be given straightaway. Otherwise, save them until a member of the group is ill, and send a card to them from the whole group.

 15-20 mins

Story time

When free play in the hospital/clinic area has finished, gather the children together just outside the hospital play area. Ask them to form a circle and sit down, ready for a story. An adult, dressed in a white coat, should come out of the hospital once the children are settled. The 'doctor' should appear to be exhausted from his or her work, but happy.

Dr: Phew, surgery is over at last but, as you can see, I haven't got any more patients in my hospital today. Isn't that wonderful? Sorry, what did you ask? How come? Well, you see, Jesus came to visit us earlier today and made everyone better. Isn't that great! You know, he does it all the time. But actually, there was one time he healed someone without even seeing them! Wow, it was fantastic! Let me tell you about it.

The 'doctor' should now settle down in front of the children and tell them the story about the Roman officer's servant, using any children's Bible. (The version in *The Lion First Bible* – 'The Kind Soldier' – is a good one.)

 10 mins

Song time

Warm up by singing 'Head, shoulders, knees and toes'. Sing this standing up in a group, and try missing out some of the words and just doing the actions.

Ask the children to show you their thumbs. Then ask them to hide their thumbs behind their backs. Use the following words to the tune of 'Tommy Thumb':

Tommy Thumb, Tommy Thumb,
how are you? *(Wiggle thumbs.)*
Hope you're well; hope you're well;
Hope you're OK.

Repeat this procedure with all the fingers:
Peter Pointer, Policeman Tall, Ruby Ring,
Baby Small, Fingers All.

Rhyme time

Use this rhyme to the tune of 'We are the Romans,' either with two voices or two groups: each telling their own side of the story. Explain that the 'slave' was a servant to the Roman soldier.

Roman: Will you come and heal my slave?
I am a Roman.
Will you come and heal my slave?
For I am a Roman soldier.

Jesus: I will come without delay,
To help this Roman.
I will come without delay,
To help this Roman soldier.

Roman: No need to come to heal my slave,
Just give the order!
No need to come to heal my slave,
If Jesus gives the order!

Jesus: This Roman really trusts in me,
He's very special.
This Roman really trusts in me,
He really is very special.

Roman: Great! My slave is well again,
Hooray for Jesus.
Great! My slave is well again,
Hooray! Hooray for Jesus!

Pray time

It is more than likely that one of the children will be poorly, or that someone will have a friend or relative who is ill. Lead the children in a short, simple prayer for the sick person, eg

Dear Lord Jesus,
Please make Susan feel better today. Help her broken leg to mend quickly. Thank you for loving her. Thank you for loving all of us. Amen.

If no sick people are known, pray for the patients at your local hospital, or sick people in general.

Extra time

•Sing the 'Tommy Thumb' song again, but this time sing the name of a child, eg

Sally Bell, Sally Bell, how are you?
(Encourage Sally to stand up and sing.)
I am fine, I am fine,
Tha-nk you.

If a child doesn't want to sing, get the group to sing:

She is fine, she is fine,
Tha-nk you

•Sing 'One finger one thumb keep moving'. Change the last line to: 'I'm glad God made me this way.'

•Invite a health visitor or district nurse to join you, to talk with the children about how they feel when they aren't well and what they need to do to keep healthy.

Adults too

Set up and organise a 'Time Bank' system amongst the parents/carers. Ask parents to 'bank' their skills and abilities, to share with others when there are times of need (usually during illness). These could be, for example: driving to hospital/doctor's appointments; taking children to and from school; cooking a meal; mowing the lawn; ironing. Encourage parents to use the 'bank' fairly, with plenty of give and take.

Top tip

For children who are ready to write, use a yellow felt-tip pen to write: 'Get well soon!' inside the cards. (This is easier for children to trace over than dot-to-dot.) Help children to hold their pencils correctly; show them where to start each letter, and help them follow the correct formation for each letter.

ACTIVITY PAGE: Photocopy page 66 for use

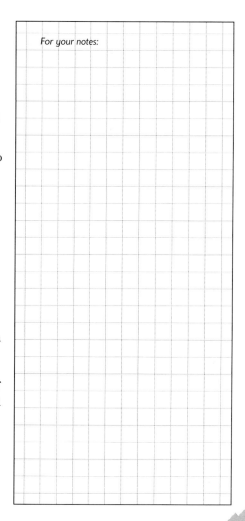

For your notes:

B18 People who knew Jesus
A man at work

Matthew 9:9–13

Play time

Shopping

Set up a shop area for the free play session.

You will need: empty packets, cans, cartons, stickers, toy money (or real low denomination coins), toy till (or tray), old purses, toy shopping baskets or paper carrier bags.

Put price stickers on the empty packets, cans and cartons (charge small amounts). Set up a table with the till, carrier bags and shopping baskets. Distribute the purses and toy money to the children, and invite them to buy items from the shop. Let them take turns to be shopkeeper. Encourage the counting out of coins.

Invite children to come and buy items from the shop. Allow them some free playtime, taking it in turns to be the shopkeeper. Encourage accurate counting out of coins. When appropriate, take over as shopkeeper and deliberately charge too much, or don't give enough change. Talk about how fair or not this is.

Round for tea

If a second adult is available, or after some playtime in the shop, invite the children to come and have a snack with you (as Jesus did to Matthew). Lay a cloth on the table or the floor and serve them, making this a special occasion.

Counting

Have a few counting activities on offer, if space and adult supervision allow, eg threading beads, counting objects on trays, or a small bowl of pennies. This will cater for those children who find it difficult to join in a role-play situation.

5 mins

Game time

Prior to the session, ask the children to bring along a small teddy. Have a few spares, in case someone forgets. Pack up a picnic basket with some simple items of food and a plate, bowl, cup, knife, fork and spoon. Gather a few children around to look at all the objects together, naming each item. Ask the children (and the teddies) to put their hands over their eyes and then remove an item from the basket. Ask the children to look carefully and guess which object is missing. Repeat several times, removing a different item each time.

5 mins

Making time

Money envelopes

You will need: envelope template, plain paper (or large, plain white envelopes, if the template is not used), ready-mix paint, cotton reels, corks or similar objects for printing, glue sticks, chocolate coins.

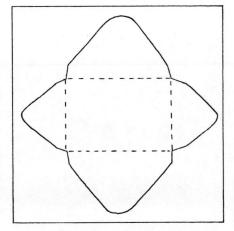

Invite the children to print freely on large pieces of paper to begin with. Give each child an envelope template, and show them how the shape turns into an envelope (older children may be able to cut out their own envelope). Encourage them to decorate their envelope with printing. When the envelopes are dry, give each child some chocolate coins to put inside. Use this as an opportunity to practise counting, as the coins go in the envelope.

15-20 mins

Story time

You will need: table with large ledger-type book, piles of coins, cloth money bags, second table set for a meal.

You will also need as many adults as possible for this story time, to play the following characters:

Matthew, the tax collector, sitting at the table with ledger book, piles of coins and cloth money bags (these can be filled with stones, just to make them appear heavy).

Jesus.

Some 'good' people, neatly dressed, with smiling faces, lining up to pay their taxes.

Some 'bad' people, untidily dressed, with scowling faces.

A storyteller/narrator.

Narrator: Matthew was sitting at his table, counting his money. (*Matthew lifts and counts heavy money bags and counts piles of coins, rubbing hands together with glee*). He was a tax man. (*Good people boo!*)

'Pay up, pay up, the emperor wants his taxes!' he said. All the good people thought Matthew was a bad man; he helped the emperor, but he also helped himself. (*'Good' people mime handing over money to Matthew and gasping as Matthew puts some money not only on his pile of coins but also in his own pocket. Matthew smiles in a friendly manner, but the 'good' people just turn their heads away.*)

They would not be friends with him. (*Matthew sulks and scowls.*)

But Jesus wanted Matthew to be one of his special friends. 'Come with me' he said. (*Jesus approaches the counting table. Matthew puts his hand out for money, but Jesus just beckons him to come.*)

So Matthew left his money and went with Jesus. He invited all his friends and gave a party for Jesus at his house. (*Jesus and Matthew go towards the table set for a meal. They are joined by the 'bad' people and mime having a jolly good time together at the table.*)

All the 'good' people grumbled: 'If Jesus

64

is good, how can he be friends with the bad people?' ('Good' people huddle together and grumble, occasionally pointing accusingly at the party going on).

But Jesus said, 'I've come to help the people who need me, not those who think they are good already.' (Jesus puts his arms round the shoulders of the 'bad' people.)

Then Matthew became one of Jesus' special followers and stopped robbing the people of their money. (Jesus and Matthew leave the table and walk off arm in arm, miming deep conversation.)

Rhyme time

Sit in a circle and say this rhyme (like 'One potato, two potato'):

One penny, two pennies,
    three pennies, four,
Five pennies, six pennies,
    seven pennies, MORE!

Each child should hold out both hands to receive an imaginary penny. The adult sits in the middle of the circle and pretends to put a penny in each hand whilst everyone says the rhyme. The hand touched on 'MORE!' (this needs to be shouted!) goes behind the child's back.

Song time

'Five currant buns in a baker's shop' (Counting Songs from Early Learning Centre, Music Sales Ltd, 8–9 Frith Street, London W1)

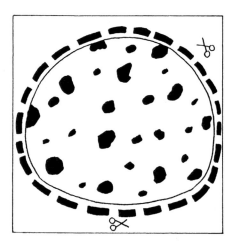

You will need: five large currant buns made out of stiff card.

Enlarge the template below, colour and cut out five currant buns on stiff card. Number these 1–5. (To prolong the life of the 'buns', cover them with sticky-backed plastic.) Give the buns to five children to hold at the front, and give a penny to five other children. When the name of a child holding a coin is sung in the verse, invite her to come and 'buy' a currant bun from the front.
Another child or the adult can be the shopkeeper taking the pennies for the buns.

If time allows, sing other songs with a 1–5 counting theme, eg:

'Five little ducks went swimming one day'
'Five little monkeys bouncing on the bed'
'Five little monkeys swinging in the tree'

Pray time

Teach the children a prayer drill. Stand up together and count slowly whilst doing the actions:

ONE… (stretch hands high above head)

TWO… (stretch hands straight in front of body)

THREE…(bend one arm and place hand on opposite upper arm)

FOUR… (bend other arm and place hand on opposite upper arm, arms should now be folded!)

FIVE…(close eyes and bow head forward)

Practise this a few times then explain you are going to pray the next time.

Dear Lord Jesus,
Thank you for choosing Matthew to be one of your special friends, even though he did naughty things. Thank you for helping him to do good things instead. Please help us to be good children and to follow you, like Matthew did.
Amen.

Extra time

Coin match game
Sit the children in a tight circle. Put a range of coins on a sheet of white paper or card in the middle of the circle. Put a number of each coin used into a small feely bag. Pass the bag round the circle and ask each child to draw out a coin and match with the coin in the middle of the circle.

Adults too

Ask parents/carers a few weeks beforehand to make some cakes for a cake stall. Sell the cakes at the end of this session and use the money raised to buy new resources for your group or to donate to a local charity. If the latter, ask the parents for suggestions, or introduce them to any missionary work that your church supports. Use any photos or publicity materials you may have available.

Top tip

Use the invitation snack time as an opportunity to encourage children to pass food to one another, take turns and to share fairly. Also encourage the use of 'please' and 'thank you'.

ACTIVITY PAGE: Photocopy page 67 onto thin card for use

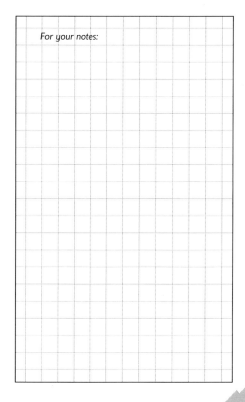

For your notes:

A soldier and a servant

My name

The soldier was sad. His servant was ill.

His friends asked Jesus to help.

The soldier sent a message to Jesus, "You don't need to come. Just say the words and my servant will be well."

Jesus said, "Be well."

And the servant was well. Hooray!

Thank you, Jesus, for healing people who are ill.

Matthew became a friend of Jesus.

My name

Pay your tax money game.

To play the game you need 5 play coins and a play person each, a dice and 10 spare coins.

Play on your own or with a friend.

Put the spare coins on the money pot.

Stand your play person on the 'start'.

Throw the dice. Count the number of dots. Move your person that number of places along the road. If you land on a coin space, take a coin out or put a coin in the money pot.

How many coins have you got left when you reach the tax man?

Start

Find a coin

Lose a coin

Find a coin

Money pot

Lose a coin

Find a coin

Lose a coin

End

Lose a coin

Find a coin

Tax man

67

Two Sisters

Martha and Mary

Luke 10: 38–42

Play time

You will need: kitchen play equipment (cooker, fridge, cutlery, plastic plates and bowls), small jugs, play teapots, biscuits, small sandwiches, cleaning equipment (dusters, dustpan and brush, broom), cushions, books.

Home Corner

Set up a 'Home corner' area with plastic or real plates and mugs. Add a play cooker, fridge and cupboards if you have some. (Large cardboard boxes with knobs and hobs painted or stuck on make good cookers and fridges.) Use low tables to create a kitchen/living/eating area. Fill small jugs or teapots with juice and have plates of biscuits and small sandwiches (see 'Making time'). Encourage role-play, sharing a snack together.

Spring-clean

Have a variety of cleaning materials, eg dusters, cleaning cloths, dustpan and brush, brooms, play vacuum cleaners. Encourage children to 'clean' the house and to 'wash up' the snack things. While the children play, talk with them about how they help at home.

Rest and read

Set up a quiet area in the 'home corner', with cushions or beanbags and a selection of large picture books. Encourage the children to look at the books. It is best to have an adult available to read or tell stories to the children, maybe including other stories about the life and parables of Jesus.

If space and adult supervision allow, have a few alternative activities available for those children who do not want to join in the role-play, eg play dough with pastry cutters and bun tins, jigsaws.

 15-20 mins

Game time

Who's happy?

You will need: twelve happy and sad faces.

Photocopy the happy and sad faces (see below). Colour in the faces and use them to play a sorting game.

Spread the faces out and invite the children to sort the faces into 'Happy' and 'Sad' faces. If you play this game after 'Story time', take the opportunity to ask the children which sister, Mary or Martha, was happy and sad in the story.

After sorting the faces into happy and sad ones, try sorting in different ways. (Don't forget to include these differences when you colour in the faces!)

Eg   blue eyes/green eyes
       brown hair/yellow hair
       glasses/no glasses
       girls/boys
       any other differences you have made when colouring in.

 5-10 mins

Making time

You can make this snack for use in your 'Play time' session.

Sandwiches

You will need: sliced bread, margarine, jam, honey, cheese spread, blunt knives, a sharp knife, cutting board.

Make sure you have a clean surface to work on, and that the children have washed their hands (talk about food hygiene). Put aprons on, if available.

Health warning: do not give honey to children under one year old.

Make some jam, honey or cheese spread sandwiches. Let the children spread their own bread with margarine and their choice of filling, using a blunt knife. Cut the sandwiches and encourage the children to share them out (or use during 'Playtime').

Make sure you keep the sharp knife safely out of the children's reach.

 10 mins

Story time

Mary and Martha share their home.

Jesus had gone to Jerusalem. It was the festival time, and the city was full of people. So he went to stay at the house of his friends, Mary and Martha. Mary and Martha were getting ready for Jesus' visit. Mary was sweeping the floor, and as she swept she sang this little song:

'Ours is the happiest home of all –
Jesus, our friend, is coming to call!
We don't have to make a lot of fuss –
He just wants to spend some time with us!'

The room smelt fresh and clean, but the best smell of all was from the kitchen, where Martha was preparing some food.

There was a knock at the door. It was Jesus!

Very quickly, Mary put the broom away, but Martha got to the door before her. 'Come in, Jesus,' she said. 'It's so good to see you. Welcome to our home!' But then Martha heard something bubbling on the stove and rushed back to the kitchen.

Jesus sat down with Mary. He started to tell her wonderful stories about how much God loved her.

Martha came in from the kitchen, looking very cross. 'Jesus, it isn't fair,' she said. 'Why don't you make my lazy sister help me make the dinner?'

Jesus told her, 'Martha, don't be so upset! I haven't just come to eat your food. I've come to talk to you. And if you both went to cook the dinner, I'd have no one to talk to!'

So Martha said, 'Sorry Jesus. I didn't

understand.' And she sat down near Jesus, too.

Then Mary and Martha sang their little song together:

'Ours is the happiest home of all – Jesus, our friend, is coming to call! We don't have to make a lot of fuss – He just wants to spend some time with us!'

Talk with the children about the story: can they remember which sister did which jobs? Which sister was happy? Which one was angry? Can you remember why she got cross?

Talk about why Jesus wanted Martha to come and spend some time with him. Then ask the children about who they like to spend time with and why (parents, older siblings, grandparents etc).

Rhyme time

Read the rhyme in full first and then, if appropriate, repeat it phrase by phrase and ask the children to join in with you. Think up some actions together.

Welcome home!
Open the windows, let in the fresh air,
Plump up the cushions in every chair,
Polish the table as bright as you can,
Lay out the biscuits, the cake and the flan.
Take the cups down from the shelf,
One for each person, and one for yourself.
Rinse out the teapot as clean as can be,
Lift off the lid, and pop in the tea.
My friends are coming here today!
Open the door – they're here! Hurray!

Song time

Ask the children to hold hands to form a circle. Then walk round in the circle and sing these words to the tune of 'Here we go round the mulberry bush':

Chorus
This is the way we clean the house, clean the house, clean the house.
This is the way we clean the house, on a hot and dusty day.

Now stand still, let go hands and do the actions for each verse. Repeat the chorus in between each verse.

This is the way we sweep the floor etc.
This is the way we polish the table etc.
This is the way we clean the windows etc.
(Add more cleaning chores of your own, or ask the children for suggestions.)

Finish by sitting down quietly in the circle and singing:

This is the way we listen to Jesus etc.

Pray time

Sit the children quietly and ask them to close their eyes and put their hands together.

This is not essential but will help them to concentrate and not fidget! Your group today may include new children who are not used to praying, so remember to explain that you are going to talk to Jesus during this short time.

Dear Lord Jesus,
Please help us to work hard to help in our homes.
Please help us to take time to listen to you and your stories.
Please help us to be happy and not sad.
Thank you, Jesus.
Amen.

Extra time

•Sit with the children and talk about things that make them happy and things that make them angry (like Mary and Martha).

•Play the 'Happy and Sad Face Game': Smile widely. Then slowly pass your hand (palm towards your face) down towards your chin, whilst changing your expression to a sad one. Slowly pass your hand back up towards your forehead, and change back to a happy face. Ask the children to copy these actions.

•Sing: 'If you're happy and you know it, clap your hands.'

Adults too

Toys and equipment always need a regular clean and 'MOT'. Why not make it a social occasion and invite parents/carers to lend a hand one evening or afternoon, to help wash, mend or repaint equipment? Provide some lively music to work to and plenty of coffee, tea and biscuits! Invite other members of the church to join you, so they can get to meet the parents/carers.

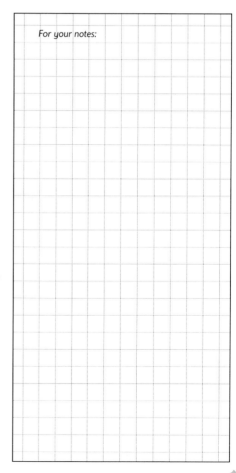

Top tip

Before serving any snacks to children, check with parents to find out if any children have food allergies or intolerances, eg nut allergy, lactose allergy, wheat/gluten allergy, diabetes. Keep a record on index cards, for future reference.

Try to provide an alternative, or ask parents to do so, so that children are not excluded from an activity.

ACTIVITY PAGE: Photocopy page 72 for use

For your notes:

A man who was waiting

John 5:1–18

Play time

Organise a mini 'Fun Day'
These games could take place either in a large room with all furniture cleared away, or, weather and availability allowing, outside. Make sure an element of fun is present; it doesn't matter if someone can't 'do it right'. There is no right!

You will need: sponge balls, large cooking spoons, scarves, ride-on toys, apples, string.

Carry a small sponge ball on a large cooking spoon, using one hand only. (Get them to put the other hand behind their back.)

Run a three-legged race (use soft scarves to tie children's legs together).

Ride tricycles or ride-on toys across the area, using only one foot to pedal or push along.

As above, but pedal along without using hands on the handlebars.

Tie an apple onto a piece of string and hold it up. Invite children to try to take a bite of the apple without using their hands.

Walking backwards.

20-25 mins

Game time

Music making
You will need: musical instruments (two of each sort), eg wood block, shakers, recorder, drum, xylophone, bells, whistles, triangles, tambourine, kazoo.

Gather together a collection of musical instruments. You will need two of each instrument for the game. Allow the children to have some free time experiencing and experimenting with making 'music' first. Show them how to play each instrument correctly, so that they don't damage the equipment. Let them play along to some familiar songs,

eg 'Baa, baa, black sheep', 'Incy Wincy spider', 'Humpty Dumpty'.

Now sit the children in a circle, with one of each pair of instruments in the middle. Hide the others behind a low screen. (A table turned on its side or a large cardboard box will do.)

Invite one child at a time to play one of the hidden instruments. Ask the other children if they can identify the instrument that is being played, without seeing it. Ask them to point to the correct instrument in the middle of the circle. The child playing the hidden instrument then shows the group whether the guess is correct.

10 mins

Making time

You will need: face template (or paper plates), thin card, round-ended scissors, mirrors, crayons (or coloured paper), wool, glue sticks, shirring elastic (or sticks).

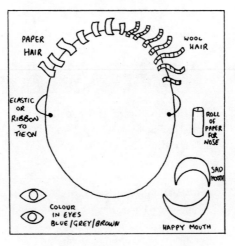

PAPER HAIR
WOOL HAIR
ELASTIC OR RIBBON TO TIE ON
ROLL OF PAPER FOR NOSE
COLOUR IN EYES BLUE/GREY/BROWN
SAD MOUTH
HAPPY MOUTH

Use the face template (or paper plate) to make masks. Colour in the faces or cut features from coloured paper and stick on. Use wool or curled paper for hair. Have some mirrors available, so children can look to see where on the face the eyes should go etc. The faces and features can be pre-cut out, or older/more able children could cut out their own. Make a

small hole in each side of the mask; thread shirring elastic through, to hold the mask in place. Alternatively, attach the mask to a stick, for the child to hold in front of their face.

When the masks are finished, ask the children to wear them. Since the masks do not have eyeholes, the children will not be able to see! Move all furniture out of the way and ask the children to walk towards an adult calling their name.

15-20 mins

Story time

You will need: one adult to play Jesus; one adult to be the lame man, lying on a bed/mattress of some kind; several other adults to act as invalids (they should be sitting or lying down, groaning and holding various ailing parts of their bodies); bandages, crutches, sticks etc to add to the atmosphere; a sound effects person, to blow down a straw into a bottle of water at various times during the story.

Set up a screen (a sheet between two upended tables will work) to keep the sound effects person out of sight, and make an area where the invalids can run to.

(Jesus enters and looks at each invalid in turn, speaking to each in a kind, concerned voice.)

Jesus: Oh dear, you're not very well, are you?

(Bubbling sound from behind the screen, as loud as possible! All the invalids try to dash behind the screen in a chaotic bundle. Only one manages to get away. The others return, sighing and looking sad.)

Jesus: (Looking puzzled, turns to the others) Where's he gone?

Invalid 1: The pool over there has special powers.

Invalid 2: Yes, it can make you better again.

Invalid 3: The only problem is you have to get in as soon as the waters start to bubble.

Invalid 1: That man made it in time – lucky thing!

(Jesus continues with his examination of the sick people and each time the waters

bubble another one disappears in the same manner as above. Eventually, only the man on the bed is left. Jesus looks at him.)

Jesus: Don't you want to get better?

Man: I've got no friends to help me. My legs don't work properly; I'm too slow.

Jesus: Get up now; you can be well, because I say so. Now pick up your bed and off you go.

(The man and Jesus walk off in opposite directions. The man should be jumping or dancing for joy, and Jesus is smiling.)

Rhyme time

You will need: *feely bag, filled with a selection of small familiar objects, eg: ball, car, scissors, pencil, Lego man, animal.*

Sit the children in a tight circle and pass the bag round the circle whilst saying this rhyme:

Pass the bag, pass the bag, pass it round the ring.
Put in your hand, how does it feel?
Choose just anything!

Invite the child left holding the bag at this point to feel something inside the bag and try to say what it is. After guessing, allow the child to pull out the object, to see if the guess was correct.

For younger or less able children, have a second, matching group of objects to those in the feely bag and set them out on a tray. If the child has difficulty naming the object they have found, let them come and match it with the one on the tray.

Song time

Sit the children in a semi-circle and spread a piece of blue cloth (for the pool) to complete the circle. Use one adult to play the lame man and one to play Jesus. If there are any confident children, repeat the song with children playing these roles. Sing the following words to the tune of 'There was a princess long ago':

There was a man beside a pool, beside a pool, beside a pool,
There was a man beside a pool, long, long, ago.

He asked Jesus to make him well, make him well, make him well,
He asked Jesus to make him well, long, long ago.

Jesus said, 'Pick up your bed, pick up your bed, pick up your bed,'
Jesus said, 'Pick up your bed,' long, long, ago.

Everyone saw the miracle, the miracle, the miracle,
Everyone saw the miracle, long, long, ago.

(During the last verse everyone stands up, jumps up and down and claps.)

Pray time

Settle the children down quietly and ask them to think about the story of the man who was healed at the pool by Jesus. Talk about how long the man had been waiting, and explain that actually Jesus doesn't want us to wait for a long time before he helps us. Then ask the children to close their eyes, and pray this prayer with them.

Dear Lord Jesus,

Please help me to remember to come to you quickly when I'm in trouble or need some help with something. I will try not to wait a long time, like the man at the pool.
Amen.

Extra time

•Play 'Kim's Game'. Sit the children in a circle. Put a selection of familiar objects onto a tray (start with just three or four  objects). Pick them up and name them with the children. Explain that you are going to hide the objects and then take one away. Cover the tray with a cloth and ask the children to close their eyes while you do this. Uncover the tray. Then ask the children to tell you which object is missing. Repeat with more objects, as and when the children are ready.

•Sing: 'One finger, one thumb keep moving'.

Adults too

Ask the parents or carers if any of them have a particular skill that they could share with the children. Maybe they play a musical instrument, or use a spinning wheel or make sugar icing flowers. Ask if they would be prepared to come and do a short demonstration session to children and other parents.

Top tip

Make sure that all the adults are aware of the dangers of carrying hot drinks into a place where children are playing. If possible, have a place out of reach of tiny hands where the adults can put their drinks. A cup of tea can still scald a child several minutes after it has been poured out.

ACTIVITY PAGE: Photocopy page 73 for use

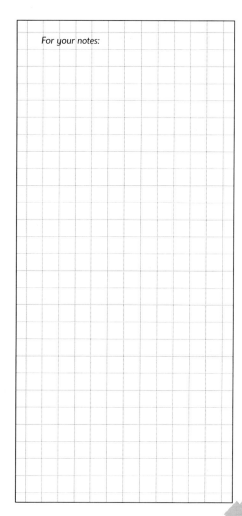

For your notes:

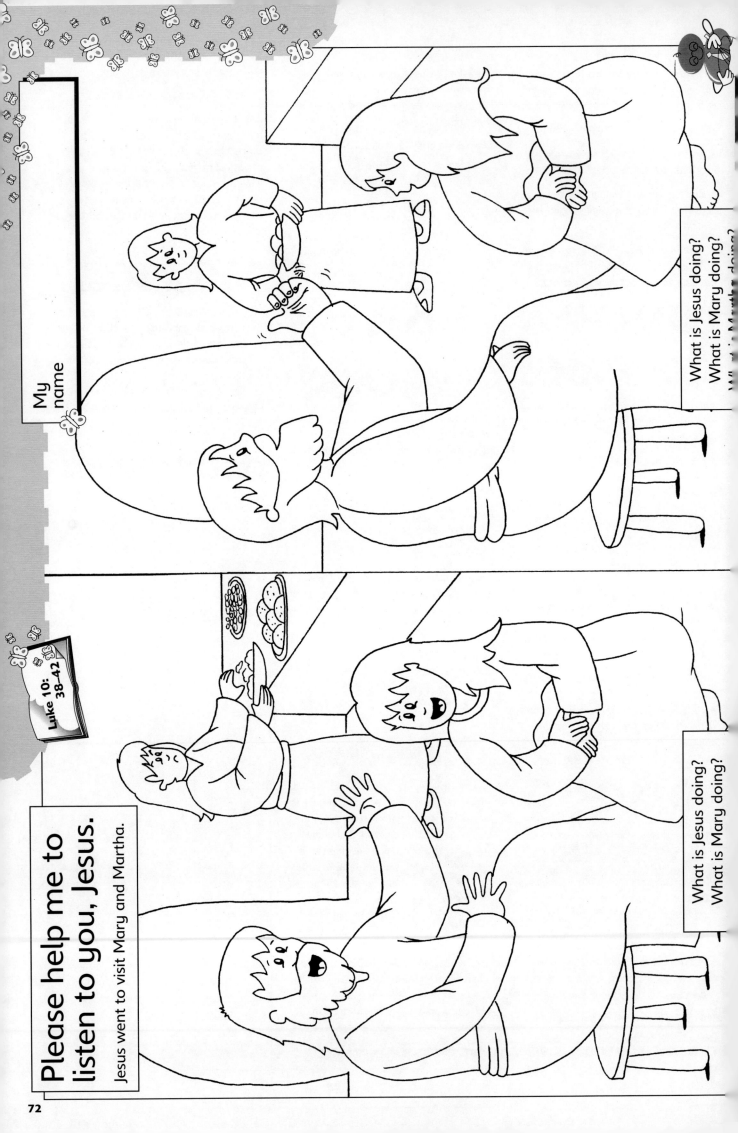

Please help me to listen to you, Jesus.

Jesus went to visit Mary and Martha.

Luke 10: 38-42

What is Jesus doing?
What is Mary doing?

My name

What is Jesus doing?
What is Mary doing?

Thank you, God, for my body.

John 5:1–18

Touch the parts of your body as you say this rhyme.

Two eyes,
Two ears,
One mouth,
One nose,
Ten wiggly fingers,
Ten waggly toes,
Two arms,
Two legs,
One back,
One tum,
That makes me
The only one!

Look at Lee.
Touch his head ear nose
mouth neck arm elbow
fingers leg knee foot
toes.

Now touch your head ear
nose mouth neck arm
elbow fingers leg knee
foot toes.

Noah

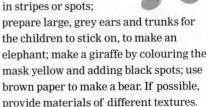

Genesis 6:8 – 8:19

Play time

You will need: *wooden objects, large bowl of water, long cardboard box, sticky tape, sheet of cardboard, sharp scissors, play animals, bubble mixture and blowers, pictures of animals, animal jigsaws.*

Does it float?

Bring in a variety of objects made out of wood. Let the children feel them and look at the grains in the wood. Explain that boats are often made out of wood. Provide a large bowl of water (preferably on a low table) and let the children see if the objects float or sink. Ask them to guess what they think might happen, and then see if they are right. As water is involved, adult supervision is needed.

Make an ark

Prepare an ark (using a long grocery box) before the session, or make it with the children. With sticky tape, stick the side and top flaps together, forming the sloping sides of the roof. Lay a sheet of cardboard on top to complete the roof. On the side make a door. Cut it so it folds down to form a ramp. Provide a large range of farm and zoo animals for the children to enjoy free play. Encourage the children to see if all the animals will fit in the ark.

Bubble rainbows

Children love bubbles. Bring in a bottle of bubbles. Gather a group of children around and blow bubbles for the children to try to catch. Point out the rainbow colours inside the bubbles.

Animal pairs

Find as many pictures of different animals as you can. Let the children look at them, and see how many the children can recognise. If possible, provide pairs of pictures of animals. The children can then try to match them up.

Animal jigsaws

Set up a table with different animal jigsaws for the children to complete. You may even be able to get hold of jigsaws of Noah's ark.

30 mins

Game time

You will need: *music to dance to, animal pictures.*

Musical animals

Bring in some lively music suitable for dancing. The children dance around, and when the music stops tell them to pretend to be a giraffe. For the younger ones, you can demonstrate! Next time it might be a snake, an elephant, a rabbit…

'Noah's in his ark'

Play 'Noah's in his ark' to the tune of 'The farmer's in his den'.

Animal noises

Ask for a volunteer, and tell the child the name of an animal. The child then makes the appropriate noise for the others to guess. The child who guesses correctly makes the next noise. Alternatively, you could have a number of animal pictures, from which you select at random (without looking). Ask the group to make the appropriate animal noise, so that you can guess which picture you've held up.

10 mins

Making time

Animal masks

You will need: *paper plates, coloured paper (or material), round-ended scissors, glue sticks.*

Before the session, cut eyeholes in the paper plates. Have a variety of animals for the children to choose from: for tigers/leopards, use pieces of orange and black paper to stick on in stripes or spots; prepare large, grey ears and trunks for the children to stick on, to make an elephant; make a giraffe by colouring the mask yellow and adding black spots; use brown paper to make a bear. If possible, provide materials of different textures.

10 mins

Story time

You will need: *wellingtons, raincoat, note pad, animal food, bucket and spade, a pair of sunglasses, a rainbow (this can be made from thin strips of coloured crêpe paper joined together and rolled up – see 'Pray time').*

Act out the story. Section off part of the room to be the ark. Start the story with the children just outside the 'boat'. Dress up in wellingtons, raincoat etc.

You may wonder why I am dressed like this? My name is Noah, and God has told me it is going to rain. I have made this great big boat… Oh dear, I see a nail that has come loose *(pretend to hammer it in)*. Anyway, I have here a long list of animals that God has told me to collect and keep safe in my boat when the rain comes. *(Read list from note pad. Ask a few children at a time to join you in the boat, pretending to be the animals, eg dogs, snakes, horses, as they come into the 'boat'.)*

I'm glad we're all safe in the boat, because the rain has started. It's raining so much that there is water everywhere. Oh, can you feel it? The boat is beginning to float! *(A little later.)* It's still raining. It's been

raining for weeks and weeks. It is hard work feeding all you animals… *(pretend to hand out animal food)* and clearing up after you! *(Use a bucket and spade to 'clear up'.)*

Oh look! *(Look out of the boat, in surprise.)* The rain has stopped! How lovely to see the sun! *(Put on sunglasses.)* God tells us we can all come out now. Do you know what he's put in the sky? It is a beautiful rainbow. *(Throw rainbow into the sky.)* God has kept us safe, and he promises that he will never flood the whole earth again.

Rhyme time

Noah noise
Decide with the children how to produce the noises in the rhyme.

Bang, bang, bang
Went the hammer on the wood.
Noah built the ark
Because God said he should.
Roar, gobble, squeak
Went the animals together.
We'll be safe in here,
No matter what the weather!
Splish, splash, splosh
Went the waves against the ark.
Noah and his family
Waited in the dark.
Crash, creak, groan
Went the ark against the ground.
They landed on a mountain
God had kept them safe and sound.

originally published in *Let's Join in* (Scripture Union)

Song time

To the tune of 'Incy Wincy Spider':

God said to Noah:
'Build a great big boat!'
Down came the rain and
    set the boat afloat.
Out came the sunshine and
    dried up all the rain
And God said to Noah:
    'You'll all be safe again.'

Pray time

Rainbow prayers
You will need: newspapers, sticky tape,

crêpe paper in the seven rainbow colours.

Roll newspaper into a thin tube and stick with tape. Wind crêpe paper in one of the colours round the newspaper tube to cover it. Attach streamers of the same colour to the end of the tube.

Teach a simple seven-word prayer, such as 'Thank you, God, for looking after us.' Line up the children (holding their streamer shakers in the order of the colours of the rainbow); then say the prayer slowly together, waving a different coloured streamer for each word. If you have a lot of younger children, encourage them to wave their streamers all together as you say the prayer.

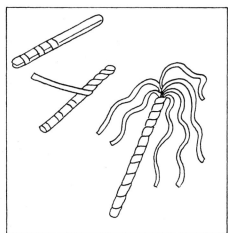

Extra time

•'I can sing a rainbow'
'Rise and shine' (*The Arky Arky song*) KS 288

•Animal songs, eg: 'Down in the jungle'

•Take in a crystal or prism and show the children rainbows on the wall.

•There are some lovely books for young children about Noah, which could also be used for telling the story.

Activity page: for best results, photocopy the activity page (see page 78) onto thin card.

Adults too

Mention that God made a promise to Noah. The Bible is full of God's promises. As a Christian, you have found that God still keeps them today. (Make sure you've got a few examples ready, in case someone asks you about it.)

It might be good to have a few biographies of Christians that show how God works today. You could leave them out for people to borrow. Why not set up a mini-lending library of Christian books for both children and adults?

Top tip

It is a good idea to collect a few margarine tubs (or similar) and fill each one with a different colour for use in collage work – ie one for red/blue/green scraps. Having one for shiny bits is also useful. This saves having to prepare lots of bits each time – you simply top them up and they are then ready for use whenever you need them.

ACTIVITY PAGE: Photocopy page 78 onto thin card for use

For your notes:

Joshua 6

Play time

You will need: *construction toys (eg Duplo, Megablocks, wooden bricks), boxes of different shapes and sizes, a brick, paper, wax crayons, aprons, paint.*

Building blocks

Provide lots of different things for the children to build with. For example, in one area put out construction toys, like *Duplo, Megablocks,* or wooden bricks. Ask the children to tell you what they are building. In an area with a bit more space, provide lots of different-shaped boxes, like cereal packets, tissue boxes etc – any junk boxes you can find. Encourage the children to build walls and to see how high they can build them.

Which boxes are better at the bottom – the bigger ones or the smaller ones? Does it help to overlap the boxes? Inevitably, the walls will be knocked down again fairly quickly, so this activity will need some supervision to stop tempers flaring! End by building a wall all together.

Feel a brick

Bring in a brick for the children to look at and feel. Provide them with paper and wax crayons and show them how to make a rubbing of the patterned side of the brick.

Brick painting

Use *Duplo* bricks or *Megablocks* for printing. Provide large pieces of paper and thick paint in shallow trays. Messy but fun!

Game time

Follow the leader

Start with an adult being the leader. The leader walks around the room doing a series of different actions, eg patting their head. The children follow the leader, copying their actions. When they have got the hang of it, one of the older children could take over as leader.

'Joshua says'

Another idea is to play 'Simon says' but change it to 'Joshua says'. If 'Joshua' says the instruction, the children must do the action. If the caller doesn't say: 'Joshua says' then they should not do the action! For example, 'Joshua says stand up tall', 'Joshua says march around', 'Joshua says shout out loud' should all be obeyed but 'Now sit down' should not.

Making time

Make trumpets

You will need: *kitchen roll tubes, plastic cups, silver foil, sticky tape, coloured paper, stiff card (optional), shiny paper or material (optional).*

Cover the tube and cup in silver foil. Tape the cup onto the end of the tube. Provide different colour shreds for the children to stick onto the trumpets.

Alternatively, make trumpets out of stiff card. Cut the card into quarter circles. Let the children decorate them with shiny materials. When the decorating is finished, roll the card into a trumpet shape and tape the two straight sides together.

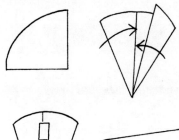

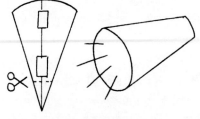

Story time

You will need: *kitchen roll tubes, cardboard boxes (or a table).*

Set up the story area beforehand by building a wall of boxes. Alternatively, use a table as your city of Jericho.

Joshua was a very brave friend of God. He was the leader of the army. God told him to capture a big city called Jericho in a very unusual way.

(Choose some children to be the priests and give them each the middle of a kitchen roll as a trumpet. Divide the rest of the children into the soldiers who went in front of the priests and the soldiers who went behind them.)

Can you see the huge walls of Jericho? *(Point to the wall of boxes/the table.)* God told Joshua that he had to march around the walls every day for six days. Shall we join Joshua's army? *(March the children round 'Jericho' six times to represent six days. The priests can blow their trumpets and you can all count as you go.)* Then, on the seventh day, God told Joshua to march round seven times! This time, the priests still had to blow their trumpets but Joshua told all the soldiers to use their voices. He didn't want them to whisper *(whisper: 'God is with us!')*. He didn't want them to talk *(say: 'God is with us!')*. He wanted them to shout *(shout: 'God is with us!')*.

When all the people shouted as loudly as they could *(encourage all the children to shout, but be careful if you have very little ones, in case too much noise frightens them)*, there was a shaking and a rumbling and a banging and a quaking. The walls of the city wobbled and fell down! Then all the people shouted again, 'Hooray! God is with us!' and the soldiers marched in!

Rhyme time

'I want somebody brave and strong
To teach my people to obey.
I'll be with him his whole life long
I want him to do just as I say.'
Follow the leader, Joshua!

'March round Jericho seven times,
But no one is to say a word.'
Down came the walls with

a mighty crash,
When the shout of the people was heard.
Follow the leader, Joshua!

Song time

Sing the following words to the tune 'London Bridge is falling down'. Add actions if you wish.

Joshua is marching round,
    marching round, marching round,
Joshua is marching round,
    all march round.
Everyone is shouting loud,
    shouting loud, shouting loud,
Everyone is shouting loud, all shout loud.
Jericho is falling down,
    falling down, falling down,
Jericho is falling down, all fall down.

Pray time

The children repeat each line (except for the last, when they could use their trumpets). Before you start, explain to the children that praise means telling God that you think he's great.

Praise the Lord!
Praise him with a loud voice.
Praise him with a quiet voice.
Praise him with a singing voice.
Praise him with every sound
    you can make!

Build a prayer wall
Give each child a large brick made up of a taped-up cereal box (one of those you have been using in 'Playtime' earlier). Ask the children one by one what they want to talk to God about or say thank you for, and as you pray for that let the child bring the brick forward to make a wall.

Extra time

•Do a marching song, like 'The Grand old Duke of York'.

•Sing: 'Be bold, be strong', or 'We are marching in the light of God'.

•The children could use the trumpets that they have made to join in other songs.

•Distribute shakers and other instruments, and let the children make a big noise (if your ears can stand it!).

Adults too

An interesting aspect about this story was that, as far as God was concerned, the victory had already been won (Joshua 6:2); the only thing that Joshua and his people had to do was receive it by obeying his instructions. Joshua trusted God, so he was willing to follow an apparently strange set of commands. I wonder what gifts from God we miss out on because we are too scared to trust him, or are too afraid to ask God and receive good things from him.

Top tip

Use *'March Round the Walls with Joshua'*, one of Scripture Union's Action Rhyme Series for under 5s, for the story time.

ACTIVITY PAGE: Photocopy page 79 for use

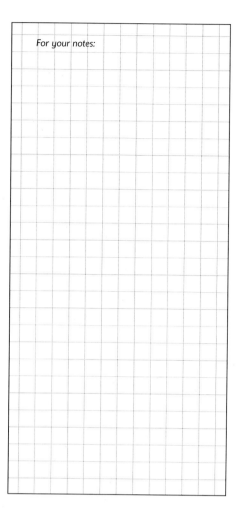

For your notes:

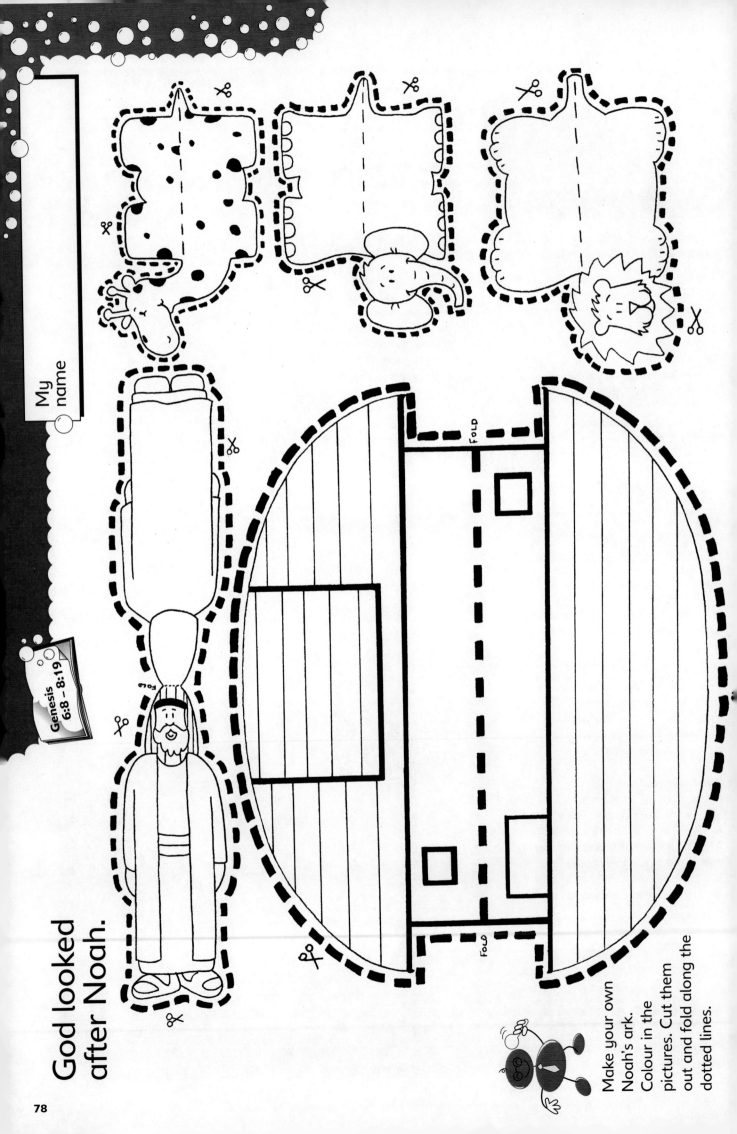

My name

Genesis
6:8 – 8:19

FOLD

FOLD

FOLD

God looked
after Noah.

Make your own
Noah's ark.
Colour in the
pictures. Cut them
out and fold along the
dotted lines.

My name

Joshua 6

Joshua listened to God and did what God told him.

Here are the priests marching round the city walls. How many can you count? Where are their trumpets? Find a trumpet for each priest to blow. Can you make a noise like a trumpet?

79

Ruth 1–4

Play time

This week's story shows how Ruth looked after and helped her mother-in-law. Set up free-play activities based on people caring for others.

You will need: Large sheet of paper, pictures of people, eg doctors, nurses, firemen, policemen, grandparents, friends, glue sticks, scissors, thin card, dressing-up clothes, doctor's sets, dolls, play buggies and prams.

Caring collage
Provide magazine pictures of people who are looking after others. Ask the children to choose the pictures that they like and stick them onto a big piece of paper, under the heading: 'God loves us to help each other'.

People jigsaws
Before the session, stick pictures of people caring for others onto pieces of card. Cut them up into simple jigsaws for the children to then piece together.

Dressing-up
Bring in lots of dressing-up clothes, eg hats, cardigans, anoraks, scarves, doctor/nurse outfits. Let the children dress up as someone who helps them – it could be their mum or dad, grandparents, doctors, nurses, postmen etc. Encourage them to tell you who they are and how they are looking after someone. It would also be good to have a few doctor's sets available. Plenty of dolls are needed for 'patients' and 'children'. Provide buggies and prams and allow free play.

Game time

Who am I?
Try a simple acting game for the children to join in. Start off acting out someone helping someone else, eg a doctor. See if the children can guess who you are. Then ask them to join in and copy your actions. Try again with different 'carers'.

Jigsaw hunt
If you have prepared the jigsaw pieces of people who are caring for others (see 'Playtime'), you could hide the pieces around the room. The children then go off and find the pieces and bring them back for you all to make up together.

Making Time

Make your own 'Ruth' puppet
You will need: a wooden spoon for each child, paper 'faces' cut to fit the spoon, glue sticks, wool cut into lengths for hair, rectangles of material for the dress, string or elastic bands.

Start by asking the children to draw a face for the spoon. Provide paper circles for them to draw on and then stick onto the spoon. This is slightly easier for younger ones to do, and gives them a chance to redo it if necessary.

Put glue on the back of the spoon and stick on the hair.

Make Ruth's clothes by gathering a rectangle of fabric around the neck of the spoon and securing it tightly with a piece of string or elastic band.

Story time

You will need: four puppets – Orpah, Ruth, Naomi and Boaz (see 'Making Time' for instructions on making a puppet). You will need another leader to help you with the puppets.
Use the puppets as you retell the story, something like this…

Naomi lived a long way away from where she was born. Her husband was dead but she had two grown-up sons and their wives, who were called Ruth and Orpah, to take care of her. They all lived very happily together.

But one day, Naomi's sons also died. Naomi was very sad and decided she wanted to go and live in her own country. Ruth and Orpah started to go with her, to keep her company, but Naomi said no. She told them, 'You have been very good to me but stay here with your families and

make your home here.'

Orpah did as Naomi had said but Ruth would not leave. 'I'm staying with you,' she said. 'I'll go with you wherever you go. You are my family now. I want to follow God and I want to take care of you. I'm coming too!'

Ruth and Naomi travelled a long way, back to Naomi's country. Ruth was very kind to Naomi and took care of her. When they finally arrived, they needed food. Ruth went into the nearby fields to gather some corn for them to eat. She worked very hard. There she met Boaz, who owned the fields. Boaz liked Ruth and thought she was very kind. He asked Ruth to marry him. Ruth married Boaz and took Naomi with her to live in Boaz's house.

Soon, Ruth had a baby boy, called Obed. Naomi was delighted and looked after the baby, just as Ruth had cared for her.

She said thank you to God for looking after them all and keeping them safe.

Rhyme time

Make a circle to form the field and choose one child to be 'Ruth', who stands outside the circle.

Ruth comes into the farmer's field.
(Repeat.)
(Walk round in a circle. Ruth walks into the circle.)
What will she do in the farmer's field?
(Repeat.)
(Walk round again. Ruth picks up grain.)
Ruth will glean in the farmer's field.
(Repeat.)
(Everybody copies Ruth's action.)
('Ruth' then chooses another child to take her place, and the game is repeated.)

Song time

To the tune of 'Five Little Ducks Went Swimming One Day'

Ruth and Naomi went walking one day,
Over the hills and far away.
Ruth said 'I will stay with you,
There's nothing else I'd rather do.'

Ruth worked hard in the fields one day,
Over the hills and far away.
'Naomi, I'll get food for you,
There's nothing else I'd rather do.'
Boaz saw Ruth in the fields one day,
Over the hills and far away.
He said 'I want to marry Ruth,
There's nothing else I'd rather do.'

Pray time

***You will need:** paper, crayons or pens.*

Give each child a piece of paper and crayons or pens. Ask them to draw someone who cares for them and looks after them. Ask them to stand in a circle and put all their pictures in the middle. Say thank you to God for all the people they have drawn.

Extra time

•Sing some songs about how God cares for us, eg 'Have you seen the pussy cat?' or 'God's love is like a circle'.

•Help the children to make thank-you cards for the people who look after them.

•Set out some activities, such as puzzles, which the children can work together on. Encourage them to help each other as they do it.

•Look at some picture books together about people who are helping – you might even like to try making your own.

Adults too

It is good to be able to value the job that the parents/carers are doing with their children. One suggestion, if funds will stretch, is to give them a suitable book, for example *The Sixty Minute Mother* or *Sixty Minute Father* by Rob Parsons. These are excellent books, full of practical suggestions – very suitable for all. There are other good titles from 'Care for the Family' available. This idea may be especially appropriate around Mother's Day.

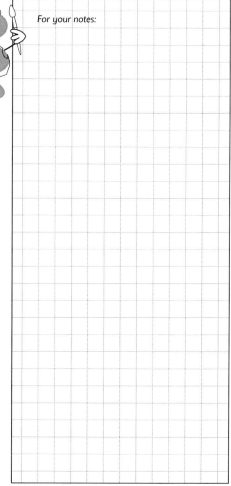

For your notes:

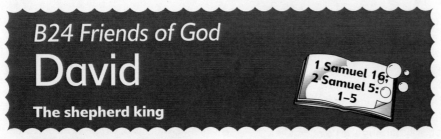

B24 Friends of God
David
The shepherd king

1 Samuel 16;
2 Samuel 5:
1–5

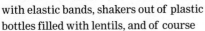

Play time

You will need: *crowns, capes, margarine tubs, tissue boxes, elastic bands, plastic bottles, lentils, card, crayons, round-ended scissors, cotton wool or brown/white wool (optional), glue sticks (optional), jigsaws, books, cars.*

Being king

Provide some crowns and capes, if possible, for the children to dress up as kings and queens.

Loud or quiet

David loved playing music. Experiment with a variety of musical instruments. Harps can be made out of margarine tubs or tissue boxes wrapped with elastic bands, shakers out of plastic bottles filled with lentils, and of course

there are the trumpets suggested in the session on Joshua. Talk with the children to see which they think will make loud/quiet noises and then see if they are right.

Sheep shapes

Provide card templates of sheep for the children to draw round on a piece of paper and then colour in. Enlarge and use the one below. Provide younger children with ready-made sheep shapes to colour in. Alternatively, make a cuddly sheep by adding cotton wool or coloured wool. Provide older children with round-ended scissors, in case they want to cut out their sheep shape.

Time to choose

Have a variety of activities, eg: jigsaws, books, colouring, cars etc. Give the children the opportunity to choose which activity they would like to do. After a while, let them know it is time to change over. Encourage them to choose

something different to do. This introduces the theme of choosing for the story.

Game time

You will need: *toy sheep (preferably a small soft toy).*

Everyone sits round in a circle. Explain to the children that the job of a shepherd is to look after the sheep and make sure no wild animals come and take any sheep away. Choose one of the leaders to be the shepherd. Ask the leader to lie on the floor in the middle of the circle and pretend to be asleep. Beside them is a toy sheep. One of the children sneaks up and steals the sheep while the shepherd has their eyes closed. The child goes back to their place, hiding the sheep behind them. Then everyone says: 'Shepherd, shepherd! Wake up, shepherd! Someone has stolen your sheep!' The shepherd then has three guesses to see who has stolen the sheep. When the children are used to the game, encourage them to take turns being the shepherd.

5-7 mins

Making time

Make a crown

You will need: *ready-prepared crown shapes made from card, cotton wool, brightly coloured/shiny scraps of paper or material, sticky tape.*

Before the session, cut lengths of card into crown shapes (prepare one for each child) and draw a few sheep outlines on them.

Give the children a crown shape each and encourage them to add jewels to their crown with the shiny, coloured scraps. Provide lots of cotton wool for them to stick on the sheep outlines.

Once each child has finished decorating their crown, fix the two ends together with sticky tape, ensuring the crown fits the child's head!

    10 mins

Story time

Act out the story, and involve the children by asking different ones to stand up when Samuel is looking at each of the brothers.

My name is Samuel. God gave me a very important job to do. Do you have any idea what it was? I had to choose the new king. God told me to go to a house belonging to a man called Jesse. He has lots of sons – eight in fact! Can you imagine having so many brothers?

I went to the house. I wondered if anyone was in. (Knock at the door.) Jesse came to the door and I asked if I could meet his sons. He sent for them. Along came the first one (ask a child to stand up); he was very tall and handsome, and he would have made a very good king. But God said no, not him.

This is the second eldest *(choose another child)*, also very good-looking, but no – it's not you.

This is the third eldest *(choose another child)*. You too would make a good king, but it's not you.

So I carried on until I had met all Jesse's grown-up sons *(choose four more children)*, but each time God said it's not him. I was a bit puzzled. I asked Jesse if he had any more sons hidden away. He told me there was just the youngest, who was out in the fields, looking after the sheep. His name was David. I asked him to fetch him.

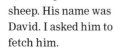

When David arrived *(ask another child to stand)*, he wasn't nearly as big as his brothers but he was strong and handsome.

God said, 'This is the one.' So I poured a little oil onto his head *(act this out)* to show him that one day he would be king. He was very young but God had a very special job for him to do.

Rhyme time

Samuel came to Jesse's house
 looking for a king.
(Hold up forefingers and move one, 'Samuel', towards 'Jesse'.)
'I want to see your sons,' he said.
(Move 'Samuel' finger, as if speaking.)

'Seven sons to you I'll bring.'
(Move 'Jesse' finger, as if speaking.)

Seven sons lined up in front of him.
(Hold up seven fingers.)
He looked and shook his head.
'There're other things for you to do.
Bring David to me instead.'
So Jesse brought his youngest son,
(Beckon with finger.)
Who loved to play and sing.
(Hold up little finger.)
This time Samuel smiled and said,
'David – God's chosen you to be king.'

Song time

To the tune of 'Poor Jenny is a-weeping'

Samuel came a-calling, a-calling,
 a-calling,
Samuel came a-calling,
 to choose a new king.
David was a-keeping,
 a-keeping, a-keeping,
David was a-keeping
 watch over the sheep.
Samuel chose David, David, David,
Samuel chose David to be the new king.

Pray time

David wrote lots of songs to God. Use one of them to say your own praise to God.

For example, read Psalm 103:1,2 in a modern version, and let the children use the musical instruments (see 'Playtime') to make a joyful noise to the Lord.

Alternatively, sing a modern thank-you song, for example: 'Thank you, Lord, for this fine day!' and add your own verses.

Extra time

•Play a choosing game, like 'The farmer's in his den'.

•Sing all the songs you know about sheep, eg 'Mary had a little lamb', 'Baa baa black sheep', 'Little Bo Peep'.

•Sing more praise songs, eg 'God is good to me!'

Adults too

So often we are worried about keeping up appearances, being the perfect parent etc. With God there is no need for pretence and putting on a brave face. He knows what is going on inside of us and loves us and wants to help us. He's much more concerned with who we are inside than outward appearances.

Top tip

Other ideas for musical instruments are:

String shakers – a string of clean foil bottle tops or crisp packets.

Rainsticks – a cardboard tube covered in foil, with rice or dried peas inside.

Cup shakers – two paper cups taped together, with rice or dried beans inside.

Plate shakers – two paper plates stapled together, with a little dried rice in the middle.

ACTIVITY PAGE: Photocopy page 85 for use

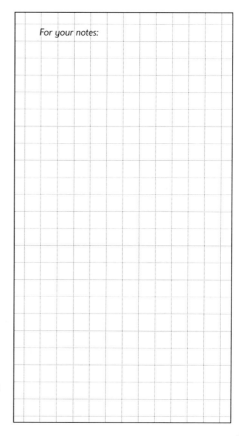

For your notes:

Ruth looked after Naomi.

Ruth 1–4

My name

Help Ruth and Naomi get home to Bethlehem. 'Walk' your fingers along the road. Then draw on their road, with a crayon or pencil.

84

God chose David the
shepherd to be king.

My
name

1 Samuel 16;
2 Samuel
5:1–5

Stick small pieces of fabric or
paper on the picture of David.
Fix cotton wool on the sheep to
make them fluffy.

Daniel

Daniel obeys God

Daniel 1 – 2

Play time

You will need: *food pictures (from magazines), play dough and cutters, kitchen play equipment, play food, a selection of fruit and vegetables.*

I like ice-cream

Cut lots of food pictures out of magazines. Don't forget to include food from different countries and cultures, eg bowl of rice with chopsticks, exotic fruits and vegetables. Suggest the children make piles of which ones they like and which ones they don't. Which ones would they have for the main course and which ones for pudding?

Make a fruit/vegetable puzzle

Take a large piece of card and lay out several pieces of fruit and vegetables. Trace round each one in pencil and then go over with a dark felt-tip pen. Lay the puzzle with its pieces out and let children match fruit and vegetables to their shapes.

Kitchen corner

Allocate a kitchen corner and set out play saucepans, plates, cutlery and, if possible, a play cooker. Provide play food and encourage the children to do some 'cooking'. Suggest they might like to prepare some food for the adults, saying what they have cooked.

Fruit and veg

Bring in a selection of fruit and

vegetables, eg cabbage, peppers, oranges and maybe some more unusual ones, like star fruit, sharon fruit. Let the children handle them, encouraging them to notice the shapes, colours, smells and different skin textures. Cut some in half to show the lovely patterns inside. Under close supervision, let them have a little taste of each of the foods. Have they had them before? Which ones do they like?

Game time

The bean game

Form a circle and move round in a clockwise direction. When you call out 'runner beans', everyone runs round; at 'broad beans', everyone walks round with their chests out; at 'dwarf beans', everyone walks round, crouching; at 'haricot beans', everyone hops round, and at 'string beans', everyone skips round, holding hands. Do them in any order and for as long as you like!

10 mins

Making time

Vegetable printing

You will need: *aprons, large sheets of paper, potatoes, shallow containers, eg old saucers, large coffee jar lids, thick paint.*

Choose potatoes or other vegetables of a size that small children can hold easily. Cut them in half and cut away portions of the cut surface to make a printing block. Provide shallow containers of thick, bright paint. When the children have put on aprons, let them print their designs onto paper. It is a good idea to provide large pieces of paper, as this is a fairly messy activity. A simpler version is to use an apple cut in half vertically – no need to carve it.

10 mins

Story time

Prepare four paper plates with four faces drawn on. The faces are sad, worried, eating, pleased.

Use the plates to retell the story of Daniel.

Daniel was a long way from home. He had been taken prisoner and was now living in a country far away from where he was born. How do you think he might be feeling? *(Show sad plate.)* The king in this foreign country was looking for some new servants. They had to be clever and handsome. Daniel was chosen to be one of these special servants. The servants were to be given the same food as the king.

You might think Daniel would have been pleased but Daniel was a bit worried *(worried plate)*. He only wanted to eat the food that God had told him was all right to eat. That wasn't the food that the king was going to give him.

He asked the soldier in charge to help him, but the soldier was also worried that Daniel might get sick if he didn't eat the food the king gave him. So Daniel asked if he could eat just vegetables and drink water for ten days. The soldier said yes, and that is what Daniel did *(eating plate)*.

After ten days of eating vegetables and drinking water, the soldier came to see how Daniel was. Daniel was very healthy and strong. So Daniel was allowed to continue eating just vegetables, the food that God had told him it was all right to eat *(show pleased plate)*. God looked after Daniel.

The king had some very strange dreams. Daniel was very good at telling the king what they meant. The king was very pleased and gave Daniel very important jobs to do. Daniel said thank you to God for helping him.

Rhyme time

Make appropriate actions as you go through the rhyme:

Here is Daniel so brave and strong,

He prayed to God all day long.
He only ate what was good;
Vegetables were his only food.
God kept Daniel safe and sound;
The king was pleased with
  the servant he'd found.

Song time

Sing the following words to the tune of 'Heads, shoulders, knees and toes':

Swede, carrots, chips and peas,
  chips and peas, *(sing twice)*
Parsnips, turnips, cabbage leaves,
Daniel ate up all of these, all of these.

Repeat the song a few times. Then add the names of different children in the group for the last line.

Pray time

Give each child a vegetable to hold. Do they know what it is called? Ask them to look at the colour, smell it and feel its skin. Tell them to look at their own vegetable first, and then at each other's.

Then say: 'Thank you, God, for all the vegetables you have given us to eat. They look good; they smell good, and they taste good!'

Extra time

•Sing songs about vegetables, eg 'Five fat peas', or about food in general: 'Ten fat sausages sizzling in the pan', 'Five currant buns'.

•Make animals out of vegetables. Use potatoes as the bodies and cocktail sticks to attach other vegetables. This activity needs close supervision.

Adults too

At the beginning of the story, Daniel decisively refuses to eat the king's food (Daniel 1:8) but then later decisively tries

to help the king (Daniel 2:16). Why did Daniel make these particular choices? How did he know what to do? Do we ever struggle to know what choices to make? How do we make our decisions? Talk about some additional things that Christians do to make choices. They talk to God, read the Bible and think through what course of action would please God. Perhaps you could give a testimony of how God has guided you?

Top tip

Don't use sharp knives near young children, and make sure you always keep them well out of their reach.

This age group love the opportunity to help prepare their own food. Some suggestions for this age group might be decorating biscuits  with icing and sweets; cinnamon toast – one part cinnamon to three parts sugar in a container that the children could use as a sprinkler. Sprinkle over buttered toast; adding toppings to mini-pizzas, etc.

ACTIVITY PAGE: Photocopy page 88 for use

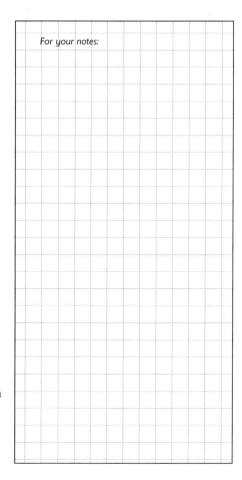

For your notes:

Daniel follows God.

Daniel asked to eat only vegetables and drink water. Can you draw him a meal which he will like to eat?

Daniel 1 – 2

First steps in Bible reading

The *Tiddlywinks* range of Little Books

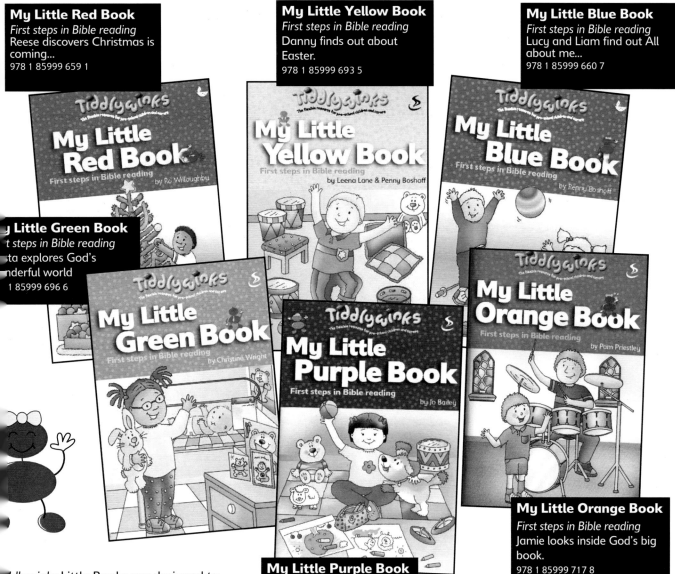

Tiddlywinks Little Books are designed to be used at home by a parent/carer with an individual child. Linked to the themes covered in the *Tiddlywinks* Big Books, children can discover and learn about the Bible and share their discoveries with you. There are 50 first steps in Bible reading pages in each book, with a story for each day and extra activity pages of fun things to do. Children will love exploring the Bible with child characters Lucy and Liam, Reese, Danny and Krista.
A4, 64pp £3.50 each

You can order these or any other *Tiddlywinks* resources from:
- your local Christian bookstore
- Scripture Union Mail Order:
  telephone 0845 0706 006
- Online: log on to
  www.scriptureunion.org.uk/shop
  order securely from our online bookshop

> " *When the Big Books are used in conjunction with the Little Books, children and adults encounter an attractive mixture of stories and activities that will encourage everybody to know and trust in Jesus.* "
> **Diana Turner,**
> **Editor of Playleader Magazine**

Tiddlywinks
The flexible resource for pre-school children and carers

Also now on sale!
Glitter and Glue. Say and Sing
Even more craft and prayer ideas for use with under fives

Have a Light Party!

This feature presents a Christian alternative to Hallowe'en events, suitable for pre-school children. Follow this pattern for a party just for this age group or use these ideas to include activities suitable for younger children in an all-age event.

Many children will have no idea about why you are having a party and it's important that you don't suggest problems where none exist! Aim to create an atmosphere which is very positive and 'light' and avoid dwelling on the negative and occult aspects of Hallowe'en. But do be prepared with a simple answer if children do ask you about Hallowe'en. Think beforehand about what you will say so you are ready if it happens. Tell them that Hallowe'en is short for 'hallowed' or 'holy' (which means 'special for God') evening because long ago people celebrated on that night and thanked God for the lives of good people. Some people today have forgotten the good reason for celebrating Hallowe'en.

Adults (and this goes for some Christians too) may see Hallowe'en as harmless fun with no 'real' occult associations. Try not to be heavy-handed about why you are choosing to do something different. Simply offer an alternative where children can come and have a good time, but without the associations of witchcraft and occultism that ultimately are not 'safe fun'.

How to set up the event

Invitations
Make the invitations yourself, if you have the time. Personalised invitations are always so much fun to receive! Design your own or copy the design on the inside back cover of this book on to brightly-coloured card. Add your own words in the centre. Ask volunteers – especially older children – to help you make the invitations.

Something 'extra'
Plan a really special feature of your party: hire a bouncy castle, an entertainer who makes balloon animals or watch a short video film on a large screen.

Registration
Ensure that all children are registered on arrival. You will need contact details for those who don't usually attend your group. A Light Party is an ideal opportunity for outreach: encourage children to take invitations to invite their friends in the previous weeks.

Decorations
Decorate the room where the party is to be held with lots of balloons, tinsel and paper streamers. Add bunches or strings of Christmas lights but be aware of safety – keep plugs and small fingers well away from each other! Anything that catches the light is wonderful – raid the Christmas decorations box and bring out the sparkliest baubles you can find! A revolving disco mirror ball will delight youngsters (but avoid strobe lighting).

Lay a long garland of plastic Christmas baubles and tinsel down the centre of each food table.

Food
Prepare some food beforehand but make more as one of the activities at the party (see next page).

How to run the party

As guests arrive...
Give each child a strip of thick, dark-coloured craft or sugar paper to decorate with brightly coloured and metallic wax crayons, shiny stickers, etc. Once all the children have arrived and everyone has had a chance to decorate the strips, an adult can tape the strips into a circle to make a party hat for each child to wear.

Welcome song
Welcome everyone to the party. Begin with a bright, happy song and ask a musician to come along and accompany the singing, even if you usually manage without.

Sing 'This little light of mine,' (in many songbooks) or these new words to the same tune:

Jesus is the light, shining oh so bright, (x3)

Shining bright, shining bright, he's the light!

This little light of mine, I'm going to let it shine, (x3)

Let it shine, let it shine, let it shine.

'Cos Jesus shines through me, Jesus shines through me, (x3)

Jesus shines, Jesus shines, shines through me!

Fun and games

If you have up to 20 children at the party, all stay together throughout the time. If you have larger numbers, organise a 'party-go-round'. Divide equally into smaller groups, each with adequate adult helpers (keep children with their own carers where possible). The children stay in these groups through the 'party-go-round' so they all have an opportunity to try every activity.

Work out a 'party-go-round' rota. If you have four activities and four groups, the chart at the top of the facing page shows how it could look

CRAFT TABLE

Make a shining star!
Have ready some star shapes, quite large, for the children to decorate (there is a template in *The Big Red Book* in the *Tiddlywinks* series, on page 42). Have sparkly crayons, gel pens and markers (make sure they are suitable for young children). Use scraps of sparkly holographic wrapping paper, cellophane and foil to stick onto the stars. Use washable PVA glue. Be mindful of covering party clothes before craft activities!

Streamers
Bind together two drinking or art straws with sticky tape and attach streamers made of sparkling curling ribbon to one end. You can wave these when you sing.

GAMES

Light up the darkness!
Beforehand, get your adult helpers to

The Tiddlywinks Party-Go-Round

Bouncy castle	Group 1	Group 2	Group 3	Group 4
Craft table	Group 4	Group 1	Group 2	Group 3
Games	Group 3	Group 4	Group 1	Group 2
Cooking	Group 2	Group 3	Group 4	Group 1

Allow 10-15 minutes per activity, plus a change-over time of 5 minutes each time.

hide cardboard cut-outs of lanterns around the room. Tell the children that you would like to show them a picture. Hold up a large, plain sheet of dark card or thick craft paper.

Explain to the children that the picture is very dark. You need some help to light up the darkness and make things bright again!

Explain that you had some lanterns, but they got lost. Can the children help you find them again? Show an example of the card lanterns you are looking for.

The children hunt for them and bring them back to the adult leader. He/she will help the child to Blu–tack the lanterns onto the black or dark blue background. Make sure that each child 'finds' at least one lantern each.

When the lanterns are all stuck on the page, hang the picture on the wall. It would be good to say in simple terms that the children are just like the lamps. They are all excited and shining – just like the lamps glowing in the picture!

Catch a fallen star...
Make a large number of stars cut from silver and gold card or thick paper. Put a metal paperclip on each. For every child present, you will need a 'fishing rod' made from tightly rolled paper bound with tape. A piece of thick wool or string (the type used for wrapping parcels) is the fishing line, with a craft magnet firmly taped to the end. (You can buy these from craft shops very cheaply.) Test each rod to make sure they work! Supervise the children closely and let them catch some stars.

COOKING
•Using 'light' as your theme, shape and cook cheesy dough to make stars, fireworks and candles.

• Make a 'rocket firework' from a mini chocolate roll with a coloured soft fondant cap and a 'stick' made from a candy stick

• Make 'Catherine Wheels' by spreading paste or soft cheese onto bread and rolling the bread into a cylinder before cutting into slices – they look a bit like small swiss roll sections.

• Make 'Candles' from thick bread sticks with slivers of fresh pepper in red, yellow or orange attached to the top with cream cheese.

• Cover a cake in yellow or orange fondant icing. Decorate with star shapes and silvery or golden vermicelli or sugar strands. Add candles for the children to blow out carefully under supervision.

Towards the end of your meal, bring the cake out and light the candles. Dim the lights if possible. Sing, to the tune of 'Happy Birthday':

We are all shining lights,
We are all shining lights,
We are shining for Jesus,
We are all shining lights.

Sing the song several times so that people pick it up. All the children will want a turn at blowing out the candles!

Story, prayer and praise

After eating and before the children get restless, have a (very) few minutes of worship. Each choose a card as you get up from the table, shaped like sun, moon, or star in bright colours, to fix on a large praise board. Add the child's name to the card; or a praise statement or prayer if the children are old enough. Sit down together near the board.

If you want to include a short Bible story, do so now.

Repeat your song, from earlier, or another favourite praise song.

PRAYER TIME

Say 'thank you' to everyone who has given them so much fun at the party. Ask the children who we should say 'thank you' to. Mention the people who got the room ready, the food, and the games – and then suggest that you say 'thank you' to God for the fun that has been shared. You may lead a prayer something like this:

'Thank you God for bringing us here today with our friends. We have had a great time! Thank you for the people who care for us, and help us to do lots of fun activities. When we go home, we will twinkle like stars because we are so excited. Bless us today and always. We want to shine for you, God. We are your shining lights!'

TAKE HOME BAGS

It would be a lovely touch to give the children something to take home, if it is affordable. Great 'Light party' favours include glow-in-the-dark necklets (obtainable from party shops/online/joke shops). Or make or buy sparkly crowns, tiaras or cowboy hats (buy at the local market or cheap novelty shop). Include invitations to your group and a little book for little hands. The 'God and me' and 'Little Fish' ranges from Scripture Union are popular with young children.

If parents have left their children and return later, use the opportunity to explain what a Light Party is about. Try to have someone available to chat to them, while they wait for the children to be ready. For safety, make sure adults come into the room to collect their child.

For your notes:

PARTY RUNDOWN
* Welcome activity – make hats
* Sing 'Jesus is the light'
* Party-go-round – 4 choices
* Food together
* Cake – and sing
* Story, prayer and praise
* Home – and party bags

Welcome time

The beginning of a session is a busy time, with everyone arriving, meeting up with friends, freeing children from the constraints of car seat or buggy, or setting out equipment, preparing refreshments and maybe taking money. But greeting the children and the adults who bring them is a time when you can really make them welcome in a special way. The ideas given on these pages aim to give you a structure for making that 'hello' an experience which affirms everyone in the group.

You could use a different Welcome time idea each time you meet. Or select one which suits your group and use that to launch your time together every session. This will help build a sense of group identity so that even very young children will start to join in with a regular and repeated introduction. It will become the signal for the group to come together, to settle and to look forward to what is going to happen next.

Your group may have a fluid start time – if so, save your Welcome for a time when the whole group comes together, maybe for some singing or a story, or before refreshments.

If you start at a set time, have an informal sing-song or news sharing for a few minutes before your regular Welcome, so that stragglers have an opportunity to arrive and join in.

Tiddlywinks Big Blue Book has ideas for welcoming everyone to your group plus extra ways of welcoming new children or visitors, saying a positive 'hello' to parents and carers, and for celebrating birthdays.

Turn to pages 94 and 95 for Home time ideas.

There are more Welcome time ideas in other Big books in the *Tiddlywinks* range.

1

Welcome time idea

I am special
Put a child-safe mirror inside a shoe box. Tell the children that if they look inside the box they will see someone who is very special. Settle everyone in a circle and pass the box round, inviting the children to look at the 'special person'. Ask the children to keep who they see as a secret at first. When all the children have looked ask them to shout out who the special person was – 'Me!'

Lead this rhyme, with children doing actions to match:

Two eyes, two ears,
One mouth, one nose,
Ten waggly fingers,
Ten wriggly toes,
Two arms, two legs,
One back, one tum –
That makes 'me' the only one!

2

Welcome time idea

Hands to greet
This rhyme lends itself to action, but in a quieter and more thoughtful way. Devise your own group actions, encouraging the children to suggest, eg what to do to 'show your care'. It is appropriate for use at the beginning of a worship time.

Hands to greet and fold in prayer,
Hands to bless and show your care,
Hands to clap and hands to raise,
Hands to show our love and praise!

3

Welcome time idea

We are special
This rhyme or chant gives a sense of group identity as well as speaking of God's love for us. When children are familiar with the words, you could split into two groups and say the rhyme to each other: first group words show in plain print; second group shown in italics; then all say the words in bold together.

Special to God, *special to God,*
We are very special to God.

Every one of us, *every one of us,*
Everyone is special to God.

Welcome time idea

4

Who do you think he saw?

Adapt the nursery favourite 'The bear walked over the mountain' as you name each of the children in the group. You may find you have to ease out on the rhythm to fit the names in but don't worry – the children will enjoy hearing their names and those of their friends. If you use this Welcome time idea regularly, have each child standing up when their name is called and all wave to them. Or you can use this song to gather and settle children for a story or talking time together: as you call their names, they move to the chairs or carpet and sit down ready for the next event.

> The bear walked over the mountain,
> The bear walked over the mountain,
> The bear walked over the mountain,
> To see who he could see.
> And who do you think he saw?
> And who do you think he saw?
> He saw Timmy and he saw Lucy,
> He saw Wesley and he saw Claire,
> He saw Claire's new baby sister Mary,
> He saw everybody here!

Welcome to new children or visitors

5

Hello, hello

Young children may be embarrassed to be the centre of attention but if you don't say anything, they may feel unwanted and unnoticed. This cheerful rhyme or song, to the tune of 'Bobby Shaftoe', gives a pattern for introducing new children or welcoming occasional visitors to the group. Use it during an all-together group time, though not as the first item, so that the new child has seen other members of the group interacting before it is their turn.

> Hello, hello, let me greet you. *(Wave.)*
> How are you? It's nice to meet you!
> *(Shake hands.)*
> Come on in and sit down with us!
> *(Gesture towards a seat.)*
> Very nice to meet you!
> *(Shake hands or nod heads.)*

Welcome to adults

6

Hello!

Be easy-going and friendly and let friendships develop naturally. As this happens you'll find you are all able to share more openly and meet each other's needs – which will not always be spiritual ones! The loan of a high-chair or an offer of baby-sitting may be the most useful and practical way you can help.

Consider setting up a toy and equipment library where items can be borrowed for a few weeks. Get health and safety advice on this to make sure everything on loan is in safe condition.

HAPPY BIRTHDAY

7

Use the birthday chart on the inside front cover of this book as a record of each child's birthday date. Enlarge the chart, either on a photocopier or by projecting the image onto a large piece of paper on the wall and drawing round the outline. Colour in the background and laminate the chart or cover with cellophane. Write on this, using washable felt-tipped pens so names and dates can be changed as necessary.

Make a plain cardboard crown and have a variety of self-adhesive stickers available. Call the birthday child forward and 'crown' them. Invite everyone to come in turn or in small groups and choose a sticker each to add to the crown, like a jewelled decoration. Settle the rest of the children down again and all sing a birthday song. Let the birthday-child wear their hat for the rest of the session if they wish, and take it home. If more than one child has a birthday, allow time to repeat the activity so that each child has a special time.

Think about how to mark the occasion, if your group does not meet all the year round. Could you arrange a home visit, with a greetings card and small present, on or near the child's birthday so they don't miss out just because their special day happens to be in August for example.

Home time

The end of a session can be chaotic, with some people in a rush to leave, others still chattering, children tired and fractious or still full of energy and reluctant to be strapped into a buggy or to wear a coat. Leaders may be busy clearing up and cleaning up. But a positive Home time can make each person – child and adult – feel they are valued and encourage them to come another time.

You could use a different Home time idea each time you meet. Or select one which suits your group and use that to close your time together every session. This will help build a sense of group identity so that even very young children will start to join in with a regular and repeated 'goodbye'. It will help each member of the group to feel part of a community – even one which only lasts an hour – and to affirm each person there.

If you finish at a set time, select a Home time activity to use as the last item of your programme. Make sure you allow enough time so that people don't feel they have to hurry off or miss this part.

If your group is less structured, choose a time when you are all together, towards the end of the session.

Make Home time a definite event and avoid having people putting away equipment or clearing up at the same time: aim to include and involve everyone.

Tiddlywinks Big Blue Book has ideas for saying 'goodbye' to everyone in your group plus extra ways of marking 'milestone' events: those going to a new area or leaving the group to start school.

Turn back to pages 92 and 93 for Welcome time ideas.

There are more Home time ideas in other Big books in the *Tiddlywinks* range.

Home time idea 1

For the week ahead
Use the following words as a closing prayer with your group. Display the words for everyone to see and as you say each line use an appropriate mime action to convey the meaning. Adults can read the words, and even the youngest children can join in with the actions. If you use the prayer regularly the children will slowly pick up the words too.

This week I pray that...
God's eyes will watch over you,
God's arms will protect you,
God's hand will lead you,
And God's love will fill your heart.

Home time idea 3

God is with us
This quieter Home time song is easy for even very young children to join in. The tune is 'Here we go round the mulberry bush'. The group can sit, stand or walk round in a ring holding hands while singing the words.

God is with us wherever we go,
Wherever we go, wherever we go,
God is with us wherever we go,
All day long.

Home time idea 2

Friends
At the end of a session, it's good to think about what has been going on and how we have spent time together. Young children are developing concepts of friendship and this rhyme gives some structure and words to express those early understandings. Choose a verse that seems most appropriate for your group or use the whole rhyme. Speak the words with a sing-song rhythm; or say each line and let the group echo your words before you continue.

Friends are kind,
Friends are fun,
Friends can talk and listen, too.
Friends can help,
Friends can hug,
You like them and they like you.

Friends can share,
Friends can care,
Friends can play with you all day.
Friends say sorry,
Friends forgive,
Friends don't sulk or run away.

Friends are good, friends are great,
Friends can laugh and joke with you.
Friends are true,
Friends are fond,
Friends enjoy the things you do.

I like friends, don't you?

Home time idea 4

Going home
Sing along with this happy leaving song, to the tune of 'She'll be coming round the mountain' and make up actions and movements to fit the words. Add further verses to suit your own group: walking up the hill, driving down the road, sitting in the buggy; repeating the second verse each time.

We'll be skipping down the pavement going home,
We'll be skipping down the pavement going home,
We'll be skipping down the pavement,
skipping down the pavement,
Skipping down the pavement going home.
And we know God will be with us going home,
Yes, we know God will be with us going home,
Yes, we know God will be with us,
we know God will be with us,
Yes, we know God will be with us going home.

Going to school

5

School-time Ted

A few weeks before the children are due to leave your group, research which school they are moving to and what the uniform or school colours are. Dress a miniature teddy to look as if it is off to school: if your skills are up to it, knit a jumper in the right colour. Make a teddy satchel from felt: cut a rectangle of material, fold up the bottom third and stick the edges down; fold over the top like an envelope and join with a small piece of hook-and-loop fastener. Add a shoulder strap long enough to put over the toy's head and hang at its side. Write the name of the school on it using a laundry marker pen.

During the last session that the child(ren) is with your group, present the School Teddy to mark the beginning of this next stage in their lives.

Get Ready Go

7

A child's first day at school is a big moment for them… and you. But while some children can't wait to get started, others might not be so confident. Making sure your children are ready to go is really important.

Get Ready Go! is a brilliant new book for children about to start primary school. Using simple words, bright pictures and fun activities, *Get Ready Go!* explains what school is going to be like, helping your children prepare for that exciting first term.

Get Ready Go! comes complete with a companion guide for parents, packed with useful advice so that you can help them get ready too.

Get Ready Go! is a great new resource for all Early Years educators and can also be used by primary schools as a central part of their induction programme.

A colourful two book set available singly or in packs of 5. Each set contains:

Get Ready to Let Go

'Have I put enough in her lunchbox?' Essential preparation for families and parents.

Get Ready Go!

'What's it going to be like?' A clear, friendly guide to help children talk and think about the big adventure of starting school!

Individual set – £2.99 ISBN 978 1 84427 132 0

Pack of 5 – £10.00 ISBN 978 1 84427 133 7

Moving away

6

Just for you

Give the child who is leaving a book to mark their departure and to remind them of the fun they have had with your group, learning about God together. Check with the person who brings them first, so you don't end up giving them something they already have. Consider giving

● an illustrated child's Bible

● a *Tiddlywinks* Little Book (Red, Blue, Yellow, Green, Orange and Purple) for children and adults to use together as they take First Steps into Bible reading (see page 89)

● a book from the 'God and me' series (Scripture Union): *Really, really excited; Really, really scared; Can Jesus hear me?; I miss you; What's God like?; I love you; What's in the Bible?; What's heaven like?*

Write a message inside to remind the child where the book came from.